Maynooth Studies in Local History: Number 50

Sir Charles Domvile and his Shankill estate, Co. Dublin, 1857–71

Rob Goodbody

FOUR COURTS PRESS

Set in 10pt on 12pt Bembo by
Carrigboy Typesetting Services, County Cork for
FOUR COURTS PRESS LTD
7 Malpas Street, Dublin 8, Ireland
e-mail: info@four-courts-press.ie
http://www.four-courts-press.ie
and in North America for
FOUR COURTS PRESS
c/o ISBS, 920 N.E. 58th Avenue, Suite 300, Portland, OR 97213.

© Rob Goodbody 2003

ISBN 1–85182–761–7

All rights reserved. Without limiting the rights under copyright reserved alone, no part of this publication may be reproduced, stored in or introduced into a retrieval system, or transmitted, in any form or by any means (electronic, mechanical, photocopying, recording or otherwise), without the prior written permission of both the copyright owner and the above publisher of this book.

Printed in Ireland by
ßetaprint Ltd, Dublin

Contents

	Acknowledgements	4
	Introduction	5
1	Background: the Domviles and Shankill	8
2	Implementation	18
3	Success or failure?	35
4	Consequences	49
	Conclusion	56
	Notes	58

FIGURES

1	Location of Shankill in relation to Loughlinstown, Bray and the coast	7
2	Domvile's Shankill estate: townland boundaries	13
3	Mullinastill House – the home of William Turbett	19
4	Rathmichael parish church	20
5	John Brack's house at Shankill	30
6	Proposed site for terraced houses at Shankill	35
7	Proposal for farm house at Shankill	41

Acknowledgements

A volume such as this could not come to fruition without a great deal of assistance from others. Chief among these has been my supervisor, Dr Terry Dooley, whose deep knowledge of landlords and tenants in 19th-century Ireland has been invaluable. Mention should also be made of the enthusiasm and encouragement of the director of the Masters course in Local History at Maynooth, Dr Raymond Gillespue.

The staff of the several libraries consulted have been extremely helpful, particularly the manuscript reading room and the main reading room of the National Library of Ireland. Thanks are also due to the National Library for permission to reproduce the map of proposed terrace houses, including the extract from the title page which appears on the cover, and the proposed farm house. The staff of the Valuation Office and the National Archives also helped with a great deal of information. Thanks are also due to the staff of the library at NUI, Maynooth, including the Russell Library, and also of the Registry of Deeds, the library of Trinity College, Dublin, particularly the Early Printed Books library, and the Irish Architectural Archive. Finally, Bray public library facilitated me through arranging access to its abstracts from the *Freeman's Journal* relating to the area near Bray.

Individuals who deserve thanks include Luan Cuffe and Siobháin Cuffe Wallace, who brought me to the site of Domvile's iron shooting lodge, and Rosemary Brown, who made available family papers. A number of others assisted through reading the manuscript, for which I would like to thank Tony Molloy, Julie Shanahan, my father Dr John Goodbody, my father-in-law Reggie Hannon and my wife Ingrid. The latter must also take a great deal of credit for being a 'thesis widow' for the duration of the work.

Introduction

On the death of his father in 1857, Charles Compton William Domvile inherited the family property and baronetcy. The Domviles owned extensive property in the Dublin area around their country seat at Santry as well as at Coolock, Ballyfermot, Templeogue, Killiney, Loughlinstown, Kilternan and Shankill. The family had not paid a great deal of attention to its property in Shankill up to this, apart from granting leases and shorter-term tenancies, but Sir Charles set out to change that by developing his Shankill property as an exclusive area occupied by the gentry. That he ultimately failed in this objective is plain from the lack of houses dating from this period on his Shankill estate, but why he should have failed is curious, given the significant number of villas for the gentry built in the Dublin area at this time. His problems with his tenants is an additional facet to the story of Domvile's involvement in Shankill at the time, and deserving of attention in parallel.

The Domvile family's Shankill estate consisted of the two townlands of Shankill and Rathmichael, comprising about 1,600 acres, lying about nine miles south-east of Dublin city centre, a mile or so from the coast at Killiney Bay and two miles from Bray, as seen in figure 1, which is an extract from John Taylor's map of *The environs of Dublin* published in 1816. The modern village of Shankill lies mainly within the townland of Shanganagh to the east of the Domvile lands. A prominent feature within the estate was the hill called Carrickgollogan, known locally as Katty Gallagher, which is a north-south ridge lying mainly within Shankill townland, its highest point being a stony peak rising to about 900 feet above sea level. Much of the ridge was heath and furze or poor quality farm land. Shankill townland also included some lower-lying land of better agricultural quality and in all it measured about 1,200 acres. On the northern slope of the ridge lies the townland of Rathmichael extending to about 400 acres. At the northern end of Shankill and Rathmichael townlands was the Loughlinstown river, and the deepest and narrowest part of its valley forms the Bride's Glen, opening into the Vale of Shanganagh at Loughlinstown. Another valley crossed Domvile's Shankill estate, leading from the north, near the Bride's Glen, south-eastwards through the eastern edge of Shankill. This valley is dry at first, with a small stream lower down, along the boundary of Shankill and Shanganagh townlands. To the east lay the townland of Shanganagh, which was comparatively level agricultural land, with some houses of the gentry. To the south lay the townlands of Aske, Old Connaught and Ballyman, which were also agricultural land with houses of the gentry and which rose up in the west into the lower slopes of Carrickgollogan. To the north and west lay agricultural and grazing land with significant amounts of marginal and bog land and which included the lead mine workings at Ballycorus.

The 1860s have not received the attention from historians that has been given to the more dramatic events of the famine of the 1840s and the land war from the late 1870s. This is unfortunate, as the period of agricultural depression of the early 1860s created tensions between landlord and tenant that are worthy of exploration. The most important source of information relating to Shankill at this time is the Domvile papers which are held in the manuscripts room of the National Library of Ireland. These include the original reports of the various experts called in to advise on the development of the estate between 1857 and 1860 and the day books of Sir Charles Domvile's solicitors for 1857, 1861–2 and 1864–9.[1] Alongside these are papers relating to a number of legal cases, including those which cover issues such as the Shankill evictions. Sir Charles commissioned a number of estate maps in the first few years following his accession to the family estate in 1857 and these provide a great deal of information about the distribution and extent of tenancies, with some of them giving proposals for the development of the land.[2] The principal weaknesses of the Domvile papers are that they are not complete and that the lack of any detailed catalogue makes them difficult to use. The papers nonetheless contain a great deal of pertinent information. Another significant primary source is a pamphlet which was published in 1906 by the Shankill branch of the Gaelic League, entitled *Recollections of Shankill during the 'reign' of the exterminator, Sir Charles Domvile*.[3] The author was Joseph Mills who, when about 16, had been evicted along with his mother and this is the only work to date to address the issue of the evictions at Shankill. This pamphlet is not wholly reliable, suffering not only from the bias and selective memory that is often found in such works but also from the ambiguity and lack of clarity as Mills was semi-literate and the text was written down for him.[4] Nevertheless, Mills' pamphlet is of great importance provided the information recorded in it is verified from other sources.

The manuscript maps which were prepared to accompany the Primary Valuation carried out in the Shankill area in 1848 show the tenancies on the Domvile estate. Their condition is poor, however, and for some parts of the estate the surface of the map is missing, along with the information which it carried.[5] The cancelled books held in the Valuation Office in Dublin commence in 1855 for the Shankill area, and give a record of tenancies during Sir Charles Domvile's time.[6] In the main these books were updated frequently and in some detail, so that information on the clearance of tenants, the demolition of their houses and the amalgamation of holdings is often provided.

These sources were supplemented by a variety of others such as newspapers and journals, particularly the *Bray Gazette*, which commenced publication in 1861, covers the period during which many of the evictions

Introduction

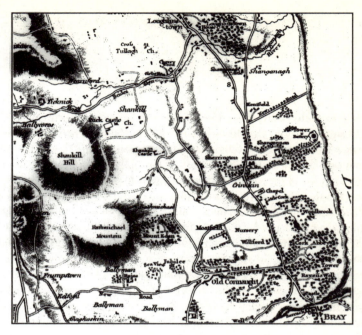

1 Location of Shankill in relation to Loughlinstown, Bray and the coast.
Source: John Taylor, *Map of the environs of Dublin* (1816).

were carried out on the Shankill estate.[7] Census records also show the changes in population in Shankill and Rathmichael townlands. Information on some of the families may be gleaned from the 1901 census forms returned where the surname remains the same.[8] Further information on these characters has been found in the admission books and the outdoor relief books from the local workhouse at Loughlinstown.[9] Finally, a certain amount of information for this study has been extracted from deeds, both from the Domvile papers and from those recorded in the Registry of Deeds.

What follows in an examination of the way in which Sir Charles Domvile attempted to develop and improve his Shankill estate both to facilitate the development of substantial houses for the professional classes and the landed gentry, and to improve the agricultural holdings and make them more efficient. Alongside these changes, and largely stemming from them, were the evictions and non-renewal of leases that led to a substantial turnover of the population of Shankill in a relatively short period. It will be shown that Domvile had character traits which were not ideal for the task at hand, that he failed to understand the property market, made unrealistic demands on his tenants and had an innovative, though ultimately destructive, approach to keeping his financial affairs one step from disaster. Through these factors it was almost inevitable that his promising scheme for Shankill ended in failure and bankruptcy.

1. Background: the Domviles and Shankill

The Domvile family has a long history, and played a significant part in Ireland for more than three centuries. The Irish branch of the family began with brothers Gilbert and John Domvile, who came from Cheshire at the beginning of the seventeenth century, and through the generations many of the family sat in parliament for Dublin and held various significant offices.[1] Gilbert Domvile's son, William, was appointed attorney general for Ireland at the restoration of the monarchy in 1660.[2] He was charged with the task of settling the claims arising from the Cromwellian confiscation of land, for which he was knighted, and he acquired an estate at Loughlinstown in south Co. Dublin.[3] Sir William's second son, Thomas, was created a baronet in 1686. His residence was at Templeogue, Co. Dublin, which he acquired in 1702 and 1703 from the commissioners for sale of forfeited estates, along with lands at Ballyfermot to the west.[4] Prior to this, in January 1691–2, Sir Thomas Domvile had taken a lease from the archbishop of Dublin of the castle and manor of Shankill and Rathmichael, Co. Dublin.[5] Sir Thomas Domvile had three children – a son and heir, Compton Domvile, and two daughters, Bridget who married Henry Barry, third Lord Santry, and Elizabeth, who married into the Pocklington family.[6] The properties of all three passed to Elizabeth's son, Charles Pocklington, on the condition that he change his surname to Domvile; this left him with land at Santry and Coolock, Loughlinstown, Templeogue, Ballyfermot and Shankill. The eldest surviving son of Charles and Margaret Pocklington, Compton Pocklington Domvile, was created a baronet in 1815.[7] He had several sons, the eldest of which, Compton Charles Domvile, died aged 40 in 1852. Two other sons of this marriage, Charles Compton William Domvile and William Compton Domvile, would each in turn come to inherit the Domvile family property.[8] Sir Compton Domvile died in 1857 at the age of 84, and his title and the family property were inherited by his son, Sir Charles C.W. Domvile.[9] It was he who was to have such a major impact on the tenancies of the family estate at Shankill.

Sir Charles C.W. Domvile was born in 1822.[10] The evidence which survives does not paint a complete picture of Sir Charles' early life, but it does provide some insight into his character. The surviving letters both from and to Charles Domvile demonstrate the affection shown for him by certain members of the family, though there are several references to tensions or quarrels and invariably they suggest that Sir Charles was at the centre of the disagreement, probably in conflict with his father and no letters to him from his father survive. The letters suggest that he had a difficult personality and this may be seen in the following examples. In one case his brother Compton wrote to him saying:

> I was very sorry to see by your note yesterday that there is still more unpleasantry between you and your family. I cannot but think that they are acting very injudiciously in preventing you joining them.[11]

Compton then offered to intervene by writing to the family. On another occasion, he wrote:

> I will do my best to keep matters square for you at home, and will make the best of opportunities as they present themselves ... I must say father seems disposed to look forward rather than to dwell upon old disagreeables.[12]

Charles Domvile's mother also referred to quarrels in her letters:

> Now any day after the 26th we should be altogether [sic] ... I do hope that this short meeting may be a prelude to friendly intercourse between you and your family. The only terms I make are that we meet as friends without reference to past unpleasant feelings.[13]

It seems likely that the quarrel was with his father, as both surviving brothers were in friendly correspondence with him, and his mother also wrote frequently.

A number of letters also survive from Charles' friend, Captain William Caldwell. While in the main these are typical letters from a friend, there is also an incident relating to a small horse given by Domvile to Caldwell. According to Caldwell's version, Domvile gave him a horse to do with as he liked, and when he gave it away Domvile sent him the horse's pedigree for the new owner. About a year and a half later, Domvile suddenly asked for it back, precipitating argument through correspondence for a number of months. Eventually, Domvile threatened a lawsuit against his friend, who managed to retrieve the horse and return it to Domvile. While his next letter to Domvile was frosty, he soon regained his friendly demeanour.[14]

Charles C.W. Domvile's talent for creating dissent was not limited to his friends and family. He joined the army, rising to the rank of lieutenant in the 13th regiment of Light Dragoons before leaving the army and joining the Co. Dublin militia with the rank of major in February 1855.[15] Shortly after he joined the militia he ran into trouble over his conduct. In December 1855 the colonel of the regiment, Lord Meath, and the lieutenant colonel, Viscount St Lawrence, were both absent and Domvile was told to take charge with instructions to make no alterations to internal management and to conduct the regiment 'with as mild and conciliatory spirit as the enforcement of discipline will admit'.[16] It appears that Major Domvile's conduct while in command was anything but 'mild and conciliatory', and the adjutant of the regiment, Captain Montgomerie Caulfield, contacted Lord Meath to complain, whereupon Domvile put Captain Caulfield under arrest for undermining the authority of the commanding officer. Caulfield was subsequently released and disciplinary charges were brought against Major Domvile. Unable to accept this, Domvile went above Lord Meath, but it got him nowhere.[17]

In January 1857 the poor law commissioners removed Domvile from the position of guardian of the North Dublin union as he was not residing within the union, following which a motion was put to the board of guardians regretting the move. One opponent of the motion was outspoken in his opposition, saying that, amongst other things

> Major Domvile had ... endeavoured to restrict the doctors from giving proper diet to the young paupers, whose constitutions were being undermined by disease.

Other speakers contributed to the debate, one expressing his 'regret for the absence from the board of Major Domvile, whom he understood would inherit £20,000 a year' as if that made his political views acceptable.[18]

It appears that Charles C.W. Domvile alienated a number of people over time, including his family, friends and colleagues. He seems to have been authoritarian and self-centred, with a limited ability to see or understand the effects of his actions on others. As will be seen, he could also be impetuous, giving instructions or making decisions and then reversing them later. This is what occurred in the instance of the small horse, and would later happen in relation to the administration of his estates and these traits may help to explain his actions once he was in control of the family estates.

With the death of his brother Compton Domvile in March 1852, Charles C.W. Domvile became heir to the family title and fortune.[19] This was a double blow to his father, Sir Compton Domvile – losing his son and heir and finding that the new heir was the son with whom he had not seen eye to eye. Ten years previously, Sir Compton had entered into a legal agreement with Compton C. Domvile to ensure that the property remained in the hands of the family, with the head of the family for the time being having only limited powers, which did not include full ownership or the power to sell the land or let it on long leases. The agreement placed the various parts of the estate in trust for the family, the deed relating to Shankill being signed in June 1841 and that for Santry following in March 1842.[20] Compton had married in April 1842 and his marriage settlement was based on the agreements.[21] With the death of Compton C. Domvile, these agreements were nullified, except insofar as they applied to his marriage settlement. Sir Compton Domvile sought legal opinion as to the implications, should he fail to achieve a similar agreement with his son Charles. The response was that the

> Santry and other estates will at Sir Compton's death pass to Mr Charles C.W. Domvile ... and that if he survives his father he will have it in his power to execute a deed ... and acquire the ownership absolutely and in fee and thus sever the estates from future title, and I therefore conceive it would be desirable that Sir Compton and Mr Charles should come to some arrangement at once ... and resettle the estates on Sir Compton for life – remainder to Mr Charles C.W. Domvile for life.[22]

The possibility of Charles Domvile acquiring the estates outright was not palatable to Sir Compton and, even before receiving this opinion, his solicitor was negotiating with Charles with an agreement in mind. Charles C.W. Domvile demanded an increase in his allowance, the inclusion of Sir Compton's own personal estates in Ireland with the family property and a share in his father's money.[23] Through the agreement, finalized in 1854, Sir Compton Domvile ensured that his son would inherit the estate as tenant for life and would not be able to convert this into outright ownership. In exchange, Charles Domvile got an annuity of £1,000 a year in his lifetime, increased to £1,500 if he should marry, and he got the right to raise the sum of £15,000 for his own use, secured on the family estate once he came into his inheritance.[24]

With the death of his father on 23 February 1857, Sir Charles Compton William Domvile, baronet, inherited the family title and property, including the residences and lands at Santry and Templeogue. There were also various properties in the city of Dublin and lands in Co. Dublin at Shankill, Ballyfermot, Finglas and Balrothery and in Co. Meath. Santry Court had become the family's principal residence in Ireland and was a very large and imposing mansion. It is more than likely that Sir Charles had decided, even before inheriting Santry House, to carry out improvements 'which were deemed necessary and suitable to [his] title dignity and rank' to modernize it, improve its out-offices and develop its grounds into a fine demesne.[25] Domvile decided to improve his income from his estates in order to pay for the work, but the rents at Finglas, Balrothery and Dublin city as recorded in the rentals did not vary from year to year, suggesting that they were governed by long leases at fixed rents, while the variation at Ballyfermot and Templeogue was very small. The two areas where rents changed over short periods were Santry and Shankill, reflecting a greater flexibility in tenure and rent levels and these were the two areas where Domvile concentrated his efforts at improvement.[26] Shankill had the advantage of a railway connection to the city, having its own station on the inland route to Harcourt Street. It also had rising ground with the potential for villa sites with views of mountain and sea.

On the face of it, the most obvious way for a landlord to increase his income was through raising rents, but scope for this was limited. Some property was not economically productive, such as residential property where the rent levels were limited by what the market would bear. Where the land was expected to produce an income, as with farm holdings, the upper limit of rent was limited by the productivity of the land based on the difference between the value of crops or animals and the cost of producing them. If the rent was already at the maximum, it could only be increased by increasing the productivity or reducing the tenant's income. This simplistic view of rents was complicated by a number of factors, such as variation in productivity from year to year, changes in the availability of alternative land or the state of the national economy. One of the most important factors, however, was the tenure under which the property was held as long leases meant long intervals between rent rises. Where land was held on short-term leases or by agreement, as was often the case with small farmers, rent levels were more readily increased. Ways in which the landlord's income could increase were re-leasing the property to a tenant who was prepared to pay a higher rent or changing the use of the property. In the late 1850s, farm land at Shankill would have brought a higher rent if let on leases for substantial houses for the gentry. A landlord could also increase his income by eliminating middle-men. Tenants with long leases would frequently sub-let to one or more sub-tenants. The total rent brought in in this way would exceed the head rent paid to the landlord, so that the middle-man had an income from the land. If the middle-man could be removed from the equation, the landlord could obtain a higher income even without any change to the rents paid by the occupying tenants.

The most valuable leases in the late 1850s were those granted for the building of villas in the vicinity of Dublin, and of these the highest value came from those with easy access to the city and with attractive locations, preferably with views of the sea and/or of the mountains. For instance, on Domvile's Shankill estate, rent levels in 1861 for agricultural land such as that held by William Turbett or Benjamin Tilly was around £1 16s. to £2 per statute acre per annum. The occupiers of the substantial houses, however, paid from £3 per acre, as at Shankill View or Springfield, through to £3 10s. 0d. at Ellerslie, to £4 13s. at Lordello and £5 per acre at Shankill Castle.[27] The lands at Santry and Coolock, and those at Templeogue, were not far from the city, but did not have the benefit of good views. The Shankill estate had the benefit of railway connection to the city and also included rising ground with the potential for villa sites with views of mountain and sea. In addition, it was within easy access of the town of Bray which was the terminus of the railway and was rapidly developing and becoming fashionable on foot of its improved

Background: the Domviles and Shankill

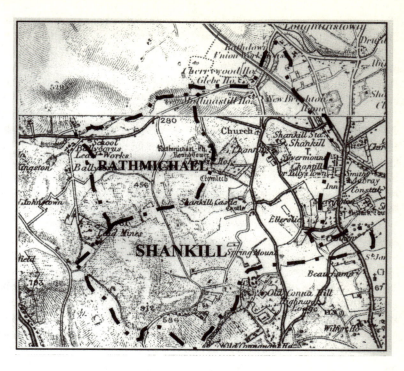

2 Domvile's Shankill estate: townland boundaries.
Source: OS 1" sheets 112 (1860) and 121 (1865).

accessibility. This made the Shankill estate the obvious choice for development of villa sites and to increase Domvile's income. Apart from its intrinsic natural attributes, the Shankill lands had been improved in his father's time. Most obviously, Sir Compton had constructed a road leading from the new railway station into the heart of the Shankill lands (now known as Stonebridge Road), and he had opened up a proper road leading along the hillside through the townlands of Shankill and Rathmichael, making the hillside accessible to wheeled traffic.[28] There had been villas built at Shankill in the past, such as Ellerslie, Silvermount, Springmount and Chantilly, as shown on figure 2, which depicts the boundaries of the townlands of Shankill and Rathmichael superimposed on the Ordnance Survey one-inch sheets of the 1860s. These villas were mainly built on the land held by Charles Toole, as will be seen below.

Sir Charles engaged a landscape consultant, James W. Fraser, to prepare a report on the Shankill estate with a view to improving the land to make it more attractive for villas. Fraser reported in December 1857 stating that 'among the many beautiful Demesne and villa sites which the vicinity of

Dublin presents, few equal and none excel that of Shankill'.[29] A great deal of the report was taken up with proposals for planting trees for screening, for its landscape effect, and as wind-breaks. He estimated that some 400 acres out of the total of 1,600 acres was high unbroken moorland, and he proposed to plant this for its ornamental effect, and to provide amenities such as cover for game and walks and drives.

On the lower ground Fraser proposed to lay out plantations to screen from view the fever hospital attached to the Rathdown union workhouse, the railway line and the 'steep and otherwise unprofitably occupied banks' in the lower part of the valley known as the Bride's Glen. In the upper part of the valley, in the townland of Rathmichael, Fraser proposed to plant a belt of trees to shelter the intended villa sites from the westerly winds and to demarcate the boundary between the proposed villa sites and the agricultural land. James Fraser indicated that villas should be located in the lower ground near the railway, pointing out that there was a dry valley here that was good building ground, and other houses could be built higher up on the hill slopes. He suggested that there was an increasing demand for larger sites and to meet this demand, as well as to 'induce the location of a better class of tenants,' he proposed that the size of sites for villas should range from five to eleven acres. When these came to be laid out in more detail he cautioned that 'care must be taken to keep the houses in such alignment as will afford to allow an equitable distribution of the sea and mountain scenery, as also to prevent the different plantations that may be formed shutting out the prospects which are meant to be common to all.'[30] Fraser subsequently elaborated on his proposal for houses near the station in a detailed plan drawn for Sir Charles. This showed that the land to the north of the station would be laid out to provide seven sites for villas, two terraces of substantial houses and a park. This was to have been sited along the northern end of the valley referred to in his report, with most of the villas facing south-west into the valley and the terraces facing south-east over the park.[31] He also suggest two alternative sites for a shooting lodge for Domvile himself. Fraser also proposed the laying out of a further four miles of new road to open easy access to a greater proportion of the land for both villas and agriculture.

In the light of the Fraser report, Sir Charles Domvile began to implement the recommendations by clearing land and planting trees, starting with the narrowest section of the Bride's Glen, between the Rathmichael glebe house and Bride's Glen House. Here he took over the land from four smallholders, Owen Doyle, Thomas Greene, Catherine Higgins and John Norton, each holding a little more than an acre.[32] Initially, the houses on these plots remained, Doyle and Higgins's being reported as down in February 1862 and Norton's by March 1863, Greene's house not being on the planted area.[33] The planting alongside the railway may still be traced today, and is shown clearly on recent Ordnance Survey maps.[34]

Background: the Domviles and Shankill

There was also a certain element of consolidation of smallholdings at this stage. In Rathmichael townland Edward Hogarty took over four plots previously held by Nicholas Hickey (13½ acres), Joseph Mason (10 acres), Catherine Byrne (2 acres) and John Hogarty (6 acres).[35] Part of Nicholas Hickey's land went to an adjoining plot, so that Edward Hogarty created a farm of 23 acres.[36] Three of the houses on these plots were demolished, while Nicholas Hickey's house, which was the best of the four, was improved.[37] At the same time, within Shankill townland, Peter Kearney, who held 14 acres with a house, and a separate plot of four acres, amalgamated these with adjoining small plots. During this rearrangement Mary Toole lost her house and garden and Laurence Byrne and Peter Byrne lost their houses and land.[38]

As will be seen, his overall scheme for his Shankill property included rationalization of the smaller tenancies, though this did not form part of the recommendations in Fraser's report. The smallholders affected by the clearance for planting in the Bride's Glen, and those who lost their holdings in the consolidations by Edward Hogarty and Peter Kearney do not appear in Domvile's rentals and would have been squatters or subtenants whom Domvile would be pleased to see removed.[39]

By the late 1850s a serious problem with this remodelling of the Shankill estate was identified. As has been seen, Sir Charles Domvile was a tenant for life and could not grant long leases, as these would extend beyond his own tenure of the property. This was a serious disadvantage, as those wishing to build villas were generally looking for leases in excess of a hundred years and were often getting 900 or more on the other estates.[40] There was also a doubt as to whether Sir Charles had the power to accept the surrender of part of a lease before its expiration date if it had been granted by a predecessor. There were two ways of tackling these problems, either using existing legislation, or seeking a new act of parliament.

The Domvile estate was not unique. There was already legislation in place allowing the tenant for life wishing to make such leases to apply to the court of chancery under the Settled Estates Act, 1857.[41] Sir Charles obtained an opinion from a barrister, Francis F. L. Dames, that under the Settled Estates Act the powers conferred by the court of chancery would be subject to the approval of the court in each instance, unless the estate was put in the hands of trustees. Furthermore, Dames felt that a private act could permit the making of a contract to grant a lease on the expiration of the previous one and he doubted whether the Settled Estates Act would convey such a power. One contemporary commentator claimed, in fact, that the Settled Estate Acts 'neutralised, as to leasing power, the benefits they were designed to confer' and stated that a simpler system was needed.[42] As to the surrender of leases Dames stated that the settlement of 1854 made between Sir Charles and his father authorized Sir Charles to accept the surrender of the whole or any part of the land and premises where there was no more than five years of the lease left to run.⁴³ He was concerned that without the proposed act any premises surrendered before the original lease was up would, during the remainder of the term, still continue to be liable to the entire rent. Sir Charles' solicitor, Randle Peyton, gave the example of Charles Toole, who held 'a vast extent of land under a lease having now 4¼ years to run and there are large numbers of subdivisions and subtenants, some of which we may be able to deal with for new leases but we have no prospect of getting full surrender or assignment of the lease'.⁴⁴ Dames's advice was that if Sir Charles' brother would consent to a private act, then this route should be taken. If not, then the Settled Estates Act would suffice, as it would safeguard the rights of the heir.⁴⁵

The Domvile Estate Bill, 1860, came to a public inquiry in Dublin on Monday 16 April 1860 before a committee consisting of the Hon. Justice Lefroy, chief justice of the court of queen's bench in Ireland and the Hon. Mr Justice O'Brien.⁴⁶ The hearing was adjourned on more than one occasion, sitting again in July 1860, before Lord Redesdale.⁴⁷ Sir Charles Domvile's nephew, Compton Meade Domvile, was the party most affected by the proposal after Sir Charles himself, since he was the heir presumptive to the estates. As he was a minor, his father acted on his behalf and engaged land surveyors Brassington and Gale to give evidence.⁴⁸ They suggested that the extensions to the leasing powers should be granted in relation only to the Shankill estates, and not other parts of the Domvile properties at Templeogue, Coolock and Ballyfermot as proposed in the bill.⁴⁹ There was no demand for building plots in the latter three, although they were close to Dublin city, as they were purely agricultural; but Shankill was different, they argued, as it lay in a district where building was extensive and land had potential for the building of villas. While they felt that 99 years was normally adequate for this type of lease, they noted that neighbouring landowners were granting 200-year leases, and that if Shankill leases could not match this, the Shankill estate would be ignored in favour of other properties and its natural advantages would not result in increased income. Sir Charles engaged Joseph J. Byrne, surveyor and valuer of estates, as his expert witness.⁵⁰ Byrne offered the opinion that leases of up to 200 years would greatly increase the annual income from the property and that the erection of buildings and other improvements would tend to improve the security of the leases.⁵¹ He stated that leases for 99 years were acceptable in urban areas, but where villas were proposed their builders tended to look for longer leases, and suggested that any advertisement for land for villas should mention the long term so as to attract the attention of potential lessees.

Joseph Kincaid, of Stewarts and Kincaid, Sir Charles' land agents, gave detailed evidence of long leases all around the Dublin area, including Rathfarnham, Kingstown and the estates of the duke of Leinster and Lord Palmerston in the Dublin area.⁵² In the immediate vicinity of Shankill he gave the example of the Hopper and Quin estates, both of which lay within Shanganagh townland, to the east of Shankill. Hopper held about 200 acres and usually granted leases of 900 years, ranging from one to ten acres in extent, and Quin normally granted 200-year leases. He reiterated the attractiveness of Shankill for villas and stated that the estate could be let for building at three times as much as it would fetch for farming; but he felt that the plots near the railway should be restricted to a maximum of 10 acres. Evidence on similar lines was given by James Stewart, Charles Brassington of Brassington and Gale, William Crow, builder, and Randle Peyton, Sir Charles' solicitor.[53] Peyton gave evidence as to settlements and leases, and showed that Charles Toole had made it difficult for Sir Charles Domvile to obtain a surrender of his lease by granting numerous subleases.

The Domvile Estate Act, 1860, received royal assent on 20 August 1860. Its preamble set down its purpose: 'An Act for granting further power to lease for building and improving purposes certain parts of the estates situate in the Co. of Dublin of Sir Charles Compton William Domvile Baronet, and to accept surrenders of leases of such portions of the said estates, and for other purposes.'[54] It contained extensive detail in relation to the inheritance of the family interests prior to setting down the various clauses of the act. The first of these was the longest and most important, granting Sir Charles and his successors the right to make leases of up to 200 years for the purpose of building or improvement at the best and most improved yearly rent, allowing a reduced rent over the first three years. The parts of the estate to which this applied were restricted to Templeogue, about 200 acres of Coolock, and Shankill. In the first two parts, leases could be for a maximum land area of 20 acres, while in Shankill no lease relating to land within 880 yards of the railway line could exceed 16 acres and the limit beyond that distance was 32 acres.[55] Clause II set down the nature of the liberties which could be included in a lease, such as the liberty to erect or take down any buildings on the land, to fell trees and other plants. The fourth such liberty concerned the digging of stone, slate, earth, clay, lime, sand or gravel and make lime, bricks, tiles and so forth.[56] In fact, this liberty would contravene the terms of Sir Charles's own lease of Shankill which reserved the mines and mineral rights to the head landlord. The surrender or relinquishment of leases was included in clause XIV of the act, but only in relation to the surrender of the entire lands which were the subject of a lease. Clause XV addressed the matter of the surrender of part of a lease and granted this power, but only in relation to the land held under lease by Charles Toole at Shankill, extending to 245 acres. No such power was granted for any other part of Shankill, nor for any other lands within the Domvile estate.[57] With the passing of this act into law the way was now open for Sir Charles Domvile to develop his Shankill estate in accordance with his vision and the recommendations of his advisors.

2. Implementation

It was some months after the passing of the Domvile Estate Act before Sir Charles Domvile began to take advantage of it. This may have been because he was serving as high sheriff of Co. Dublin, a position which carried significant responsibilities, including execution of legal processes of the courts such as eviction notices, and the appointment of the grand juries, who had responsibility for works such as the building and maintenance of roads and bridges. Sir Charles brought his own element of pageantry to the office, reviving, according to the *London Morning Chronicle*, 'some old, respectable, but obsolete customs pertaining to that ancient and honourable office'.[1] At the opening of the Easter term in the courts, Sir Charles provided breakfast for 400 of his tenants in a large marquee on the lawn of Santry Court. After breakfast they set off in a cavalcade led by his servants, dressed in the family livery and mounted on horses, followed by 300 tenants who preceded Sir Charles himself riding in a landau flanked by four outriders, and at the rear were 100 gentleman tenants on horseback. This procession, watched by a great crowd, led Sir Charles to the Four Courts, where he was present for the swearing of the grand juries.[2] Domvile then treated his tenants to a banquet in the Rotunda, and in the evening he held another banquet at Santry Court for 70 people, including nearly all of the judges and a large number of the nobility and gentry. On the following day Santry was the venue for a ball to which he invited up to 1,500 people.[3] The *London Morning Chronicle* commented that 'you observe the revival of the custom is not unattended with expense'.[4] Phineas Riall, whose property adjoined Domvile's Shankill estate, was less reserved in his comment, recording in his diary that he went in to town to:

> see the Sheriff Sir Chas. C. Domvile make a fool of himself which he did in perfection, he drove in procession with his tenantry and oh such a set and such a cortege a pen fails to describe.[5]

Domvile began renewed activity on his Shankill estate in January 1861 when he served notices to quit on two tenants, Benjamin Tilly and Felix Hughes.[6] These were not small tenants. Tilly was a solicitor living in a substantial house on more than 60 acres in Shankill; he also held more than a 100 acres elsewhere in the townland and about 45 acres in the adjoining townland of Shanganagh where he owned three substantial houses let to

Implementation

3 Mullinastill House – the home of William Turbett.

tenants.[7] Felix Hughes was a farmer in the townland of Rathmichael, where he held almost a 100 acres and 14 acres in the adjoining townland of Ballycorus.[8] The service of these notices was purely tactical, however, to give Domvile's solicitor Randle Peyton a better negotiating position.[9]

These were not Sir Charles' first threats to evict. In 1858 he had sought the ejectment of a 'pauper tenant' for non-payment of rent. Three weeks later he sought to evict William Turbett, a farmer of 100 acres at Shankill, as his lease had expired, though Turbett immediately put forward a proposal for a new lease.[10] He remained in his home at Mullinastill House (shown in figure 3) for only a short period after this. Another tenant to be threatened was the Mining Company of Ireland, which had substantial lead works in the adjoining townland of Ballycorus and had taken a lease from Sir Charles' father in 1845 of 36 acres in Rathmichael townland. Sir Charles discovered that in contravention of the lease there were four houses on this land, including one with a forge, and he demanded the very high rate of £8 per acre for all the lands held.[11] He later evicted the mining company and the four tenants whose houses were demolished.[12]

Actions such as this made it clear that Sir Charles Domvile was going to adopt a no-nonsense approach to his property and the terms of leases or agreements. This attitude extended to all users of his land and not just tenants, as is illustrated in stories which appeared in the newspapers from time to time.

4 Rathmichael parish church.

For instance, the *Bray Gazette* reported in January 1862 on a case by Domvile before Bray petty sessions which related to an alleged trespass the previous November when 'the proprietor of a college or seminary' had taken ten of his pupils to see the ruins of Rathmichael church, an early-Christian church site of some local archaeological importance. A 'mitigated fine' of six pence was imposed.[13] In a similar case, Sir Charles prosecuted another teacher for taking pupils to see Puck's Castle in Rathmichael.[14] In October 1862, another four people found themselves before Bray petty sessions on Sir Charles' suit. Two women were charged with cutting grass in Sir Charles' plantation at Shankill without his permission, one being fined 6*d*. the other case being dismissed. At the same time two workmen were sued by Sir Charles for allegedly taking limestone from his estate without permission, but both cases were dismissed.[15]

One of the more positive moves made by Domvile was to proceed with the provision of a Church of Ireland parish church at Shankill. The parish of Rathmichael had been without its own church since the early 17th century, and its small but significant congregation had worshipped in Bray.[16] Sir Charles realized that if land was leased for the building of villas many of the occupiers would be of the anglican faith and the existence of a parish church would signal that the area was up-and-coming, while also providing a place of worship for these occupiers. In April 1858 he indicated that he would provide the ground for a parish church as well as £100, later deciding to build the church at his own expense.¹⁷ Domvile conveyed one statute acre to the parish of Rathmichael and in this deed the reasons given for Domvile's beneficence were that he was 'desirous to grant ... a site for a church ... in order to effectuate such his intent for the promotion of religion and service of God' and 'for the good will he bears the inhabitants of [Rathmichael] parish.'¹⁸ No mention was made of improving the attractiveness of the district to potential lessees.

The task of designing the new church was given to the architects Deane and Woodward and they were already working on the plans by the time the land was conveyed to the parish. It appears that the initial designs were done by Benjamin Woodward, but Woodward's early death ensured that the design was finalized by Thomas Newenham Deane.¹⁹ In March 1861 Deane proposed that Gilbert Cockburne should be engaged to build the church, but Sir Charles preferred that the job be given to Messrs Carolin, who were working on his home at Santry. He also wanted them to build two houses at Shankill.²⁰ In fact, Carolin declined the commission.²¹ The job was put out to tender, the successful bidder being James Douglass, who quoted £700.²²

As plans were finalized and preparations for building were made, James Douglass sought permission to quarry for stones locally.²³ Sir Charles then engaged the well-known geologist James Beete Jukes, of the Geological Survey of Ireland, to advise on the probability of finding brick clay, lime and sand at Shankill.²⁴ None of these emerged from the search, and it was found necessary to bring materials from further afield.²⁵

The building of the church began in 1862 and completed in the following year.²⁶ Phineas Riall visited the church during construction and was not impressed, writing in his diary that it was 'the poorest Parish Church I ever saw – miserably small & no ornament whatever, a poor creation for Domvile purse & family.'²⁷ Sir Charles had opted for a parish church to seat just 100 people, which was hardly an expression of confidence in the future growth of the population of the district. In fact, despite Domvile's failure to develop villas on his lands, the church needed to be doubled in size just five years after its consecration, and it was enlarged again in 1904 to take on the appearance shown in figure 4.²⁸ The incumbent of Rathmichael, the Revd John Hunt, died just two years after the church was opened, but it is probable that he never saw it. Phineas Riall recorded that Hunt had died 'rather suddenly if it could be so said when he was nearly six years paralized and confined to bed.'²⁹ Small though the church was, Sir Charles Domvile ensured that he and his family, past and present, were treated well. Mrs Turner, in her history of Rathmichael parish recorded that

> Half-way up the nave, opposite the south door was the Domvile pew, enclosed in red velvet curtains, with a settee and two high-backed chairs covered in the same red velvet, occupied by Sir Charles Domvile

on Sundays when he came over from Santry Court. The only memorial windows were, of course, Domvile ones. 'Christ stepping from the Tomb', dedicated to Sir Charles's parents ... was then the east window in the chancel, flanked by two other Domvile windows now in the vestry room. Two brass memorial tablets inside the west door record the names of the family from 1615 on, and that they are interred in St Patrick's Cathedral ... A circular window at the west end of the north aisle depicts the family coat of arms.[30]

The sumptuous accommodation which Sir Charles provided for himself in the parish church signals that he intended to appear regularly on his Shankill estate. The Domviles had never lived at Shankill, and the lavish expenditure on improvements at Santry Court show that Sir Charles had no intention of making Shankill his permanent residence, but he nonetheless built himself a shooting lodge there. Information about this house, its designers, the dates of construction and so forth are scanty in the Domvile papers, but a few facts may be gleaned from that source and elsewhere. Sir Charles selected a site on high ground at the southern end of the property and with exceptionally fine views.[31] To provide a substantial demesne for the house he set about acquiring possession of land for the shooting lodge from his tenants, principally Phineas Riall, who rented land adjoining his demesne at Old Conna Hill, and Patrick McAneny, who held 38 acres adjoining Riall's demesne.[32] With smaller plots from Jane Mason, Mary Burke and William Woods, the total site for the new demesne was brought to 93 acres.[33]

The house that was erected was first valued in February 1862 when the valuation inspector described it as 'Summer lodge built of iron.'[34] Phineas Riall mentioned a visit to 'Mr Domvile's extraordinary buildings', and later he visited 'Sir C Domvile's buildings – curious samples of architecture'.[35] In 1861 and again in 1862, quantity surveyor Benjamin Patterson visited the site to measure the works 'at Shankill shooting lodge'.[36] Buildings of glass and iron had become popular, particularly for horticultural or botanical purposes, the larger examples of which included Richard Turner's curvilinear range at the Botanic Gardens in Dublin (1840s) and Paxton's Crystal Palace (1851). However, it seems unlikely that Domvile's shooting lodge was of this type as it would then have been described in a way that suggested glass or crystal. It is more likely that the building was made from sheet iron, most probably corrugated iron. This material had been invented in 1828 and became more useful after the development of galvanizing in 1837.[37] It began to be used widely for the construction of entire buildings rather than just roofs in the 1850s, and by the 1860s was available as barn-type structures or more domestic-scale buildings. The latter could be formed using a light timber frame clad with iron, and could be produced in a variety of sizes and styles.[38] Sir Charles Domvile used iron on buildings elsewhere on his property, particularly at Santry. The architectural drawings for his new building work include plans for a farm house of traditional construction, except that the internal partition walls were of iron.[39] Another drawing, depicting the stable yard, shows a canopy running to the front of the stables, and this is clearly made from corrugated iron.[40] More particularly, Domvile had a farm house of corrugated iron built at Racefields on the Santry estate.[41] This was a relatively plain building 20 feet square, but with wavy decorative bargeboards at the gables as was often found in farmhouses of more traditional materials on model estates of the period.[42] These buildings were provided by Morton of Liverpool, who also supplied him with galvanized iron fencing, a kennel, a riding school and drying houses.[43]

Sir Charles stayed in his new house at Shankill in August 1862, when the *Bray Gazette* commented:

> Sir C. Domvile bt. has arrived at Shankhill (sic) and occupies an iron house of considerable dimensions situated on the southern slope of the hill. He remains in the locality for a month for the enjoyment of the shooting season which is unusually good, not only in that district, but in various parts of Co. Wicklow.[44]

The house was ready for occupation, but had not yet been landscaped. While he was at the house, he wrote a number of letters to the eminent landscape gardener, Ninian Niven, requesting designs for the landscaping of the house and demesne.[45] Niven is more usually associated with the typically-Victorian public park such as the People's Gardens in the Phoenix Park, Blackrock Park, Co. Dublin, and the gardens of the Royal Marine Hotel in Kingstown (Dun Laoghaire).[46] When he designed the gardens of large houses he included a similar repertoire of bedding plants, fountains, walks, lawns and, typically, the Irish yew. His work at Killakee House in the Dublin mountains is well-known, however, and the terrain has similarities to that at Shankill, on an elevated site with fine views at the foot of more rugged mountain land. Niven proposed to plant the higher ground with trees for shelter, to give a pleasant backdrop to the house and to provide cover for game.[47] The final touch to the lodge was the construction of a coach house which Sir Charles seems to have added as an extra, asking the builder, James Douglass, in a fairly casual way to erect one, the price being settled by having it measured by the quantity surveyor Benjamin Patterson.[48]

The construction of the parish church and Domvile's offer to act as the equivalent of an anchor tenant by building his own house was not in itself sufficient to ensure that sites would be developed for villas. Fraser's report had identified areas where villas should be sited, but this property was already in lease and so the Domvile Estate Act, 1860 was needed to bring this to fruition. Charles Toole, a nurseryman based in Dublin's Westmoreland Street, held a large tract of land under two leases which amounted to the majority of the lowland regions of Shankill townland. As a great deal of the townland consisted of uplands with poor soil and not suitable for villas, Toole's land was important if new houses for the gentry were to be built. The amount of Toole's rent may have reflected the fact that the leases did not preclude building or subletting, provided, of course, it was for a period not longer than the duration of the Tooles' own lease, and the Tooles did, in fact, supplement their income from the nursery business by building houses or leasing land for house-building. This included the substantial houses of Sylvan Mount, on almost five Irish acres, leased in 1809,[49] and a house called Shankill, on more than 10 Irish acres, leased to solicitor Robert Maddock in 1812,[50] as well as farm land leased to Margaret Behan in 1809.[51] The Tooles had found a way around the problem that their leases were too short to encourage potential builders of substantial houses. Each lease included a clause undertaking to grant a longer one in the event of their taking a new lease from the Domviles. With this technique, a significant amount of house-building took place on Toole's Shankill lands in the 1820s and 1830s with the building of Lordello, Springfield, Ellerslie, Chantilly and Rathmichael Lodge.[52] The Toole leases had been renewed for twenty years from 1844.

Sir Charles Domvile seems to have decided at an early stage that he should seek the surrender of the Toole lease. In March 1858 his solicitor, Randle Peyton, called up a copy and was instructed to have the buildings on Toole's land inspected, though not much was done at this stage pending the passing of the Domvile Estate Act.[53] The process began in earnest in March 1861, when Peyton was instructed to enter into negotiations with Toole for the purchase of his interest.[54] Toole's initial response was to offer to surrender his lease and the 92 acres which he held directly, for £2,000, and to take 34 acres back as building ground, though Peyton considered that not more than £1,000 should be paid. They settled on £1,375 plus the cost of seed and labour expended on the crops then growing, subject to no claims being made in respect of the repair of buildings. This was to be paid in instalments, and was the full amount of the rent which he would have got had his lease been let run its full course, plus £3 14s. per acre per year for his own holding.[55] This was generous on two counts. First, it ensured that he was paid regardless of whether each holding was occupied. Secondly, he was given a generous annual value for his 92 acres. The majority of his own tenants were paying less than this, £3 2s. being the average paid by Mrs Butler, Miss Gernon, J. W. Mackey and Henry Purcell.[56] Others paid less, such as Peter Jackson who paid only £2 1s. The land occupied by those tenants was in the vicinity of Toole's 92 acres and would not differ much in quality from it. Moreover, their rent was at housing values, whereas Toole had no houses on his holding, and agricultural values would have been closer to the £1 17s. an Irish acre that Benjamin Tilly was paying.[57] A further potential benefit to Toole was that he

Implementation

was freed from the cost, uncertainty and trouble of collecting his rents. However, given that the payment was to be made in instalments these issues would remain, though in a single payment. As will be shown, Sir Charles Domvile was not a reliable and certain debtor. For Sir Charles' part, he was willing to pay this price as it allowed him to regain control of the land. He would then be in a position to renegotiate the leases of the existing tenants, presumably at higher rents, and he would hope to grant other building leases to further increase his income from the lands.

There were a few delays in the completion of the deal. The draft deed of conveyance was prepared immediately, and the final deed was completed five months later on 7 August 1861, just over two and a half years left before the expiry of the lease, to 25 March 1864. This transferred the two tracts of land held by Toole to William Charles Caldwell (the same William Caldwell with whom Domvile had had the disagreement over the horse ten years previously). Caldwell was to hold it in trust for Sir Charles for the remainder of the terms of Toole's leases.[58] The existence of so many subtenants on the Toole lands complicated matters. The lists showed that Charles Toole had 16 tenants, and of these four held houses valued at more than £30, while a further three had houses worth £15 or more.[59] Some of these tenants were further subletting their properties, such as Andrew Tracy, who held less than three acres and a house valued at £2 had no less than six tenants of his own, each occupying a modest house.[60] Each subtenant had rights only as long as the principal tenant's lease remained unexpired and, naturally, their under-tenants were in the same position. Sir Charles was now in a position to carry out any consolidation or other improvements he wished on the land, and to renegotiate leases.

In his pamphlet on the Domvile evictions, Joseph Mills mentioned the names of those whom he claimed were evicted by Sir Charles Domvile including those evicted as a result of his acquisition of the Toole lease. Amongst the names are eight of the 16 former tenants of Charles Toole, as well as four of their subtenants.[61] Taking the names from Toole's list of May 1861, these were Mrs Byrne, Mrs Butler, H. Purcell, Benjamin Tilly, Edward Thomas, Mrs Tracey, P. Toole and M. Toole.[62] It has already been pointed out that Benjamin Tilly was served notice to quit in January 1861. Tilly's holding included some land leased from Charles Toole and more from Sir Charles Domvile, in addition to the land across the townland boundary into Shanganagh.[63] Over the ensuing months Randle Peyton conducted negotiations with Tilly, including an offer of a two-hundred year lease.[64] In August 1861, Joseph Kincaid, the land surveyor who advised Sir Charles, suggested that £120 per year would be a reasonable rent on Tilly's house, 'Chantilly', a figure which was only marginally above the £114 10s. 2d. that Tilly had been paying to Charles Toole.[65] Tilly was willing to accept this initially and over the next five months negotiations continued, until in January 1862 Domvile directed that Benjamin Tilly should be put out of his holding.[66] This concentrated the negotiations for a short period, but they did not move fast enough and at the beginning of April Domvile instructed his solicitor that unless the arrangements were completed by the following Monday they were to be broken off.[67] Benjamin Tilly's response was that he would not take the premises because the terms of the proposed lease were unreasonably stringent.[68] The valuation records show that Tilly no longer held the northern portion of his Shankill lands by February 1862, and subsequent to this, and prior to March 1864 he had left Chantilly and its lands.[69]

Domvile's solution to the problem of subtenants was eviction, and on 20 March 1862 his agent requested that notices to quit be served on Toole's subtenants.[70] Charles Toole's leasing power could only be for the duration of his own leases and once they had been surrendered Toole's tenants would have to renegotiate with Domvile or quit the properties. There were 14 tenants of Charles Toole who, between them, had some 17 subtenants at the time of the surrender of Toole's lease. Within three years, 15 of the houses of subtenants had been demolished or were vacant or derelict, the exception being the two subtenants of Peter Toole whose houses were substantial and which survive today as Rathmichael Lodge and Woodford on Ballybride Road. In addition, the houses of Toole's smaller tenants belonging to Henry Purcell, Edward Thomas, Mrs Tracy and Margaret Toole suffered the same fate. Miss Gernon's house was large enough to have a name, Aughmore, but this did not save it from demolition. Where the houses were not vacated or demolished, the occupiers changed, so that in a short time not one of Toole's tenants or their subtenants remained in place.[71] In the case of the larger of Toole's tenants it is probable that some of them moved out of their own accord. Domvile's solicitor had extensive negotiations with Benjamin Tilly, but apparently not in other cases on Toole's land. In November 1861 Sir Charles directed his solicitor to inform Toole's tenants J.W. Mackey, Dr. Biggar and the Revd. Mr Hackett that new arrangements were to be made.[72] However, except for James Mackey's attempt to acquire a lease of Ballybride there is no mention of negotiations over leases.[73] Domvile's rentals mention in September 1864 that Mrs Butler and Edward Thomas were ejected from their holdings.[74]

The lands held by Charles Toole and the adjoining land held by Benjamin Tilly were important to Sir Charles Domvile, occupying some of the finest land on the Shankill estate and having good sea and mountain views that made them attractive for development – including the 'fine deep central glen' to which James Fraser had referred in his report.[75] Although Toole's lands contained just 240 acres out of a total of about 1,600 in Shankill and Rathmichael, many of the existing villas and substantial houses on the estate were on this part of the property, including Chantilly, Shankill Lodge, Emerald, Silvermount (later Sylvan Mount), Springfield, Ballybride, Shankill (demolished), Aughmore, Ellerslie, Lordello and Spring Mount. This contrasts with the remainder of the estate on which the only substantial houses were Mullinastill, Shankill House, Shanganagh Cottage (later Ferndale) and Shankill Castle.[76]

Sir Charles did not confine his attentions to Toole's lands though and sought to improve the value of the entire holding. On the remainder of the Shankill estate there were 71 houses, including two gate lodges, at the time that Sir Charles inherited the property.[77] There were some tenants who did not live on the Domvile estate. Of the remainder, there were seven tenants who held more than 20 acres each, excluding Benjamin Tilly. The most significant tenants, in terms of acreage or size of house, were:

Name	Acreage	Townland	Property
Felix Hughes	99a 3r 7p	Rathmichael	
James Dolan	25a 1r 2p	Rathmichael	
Michael Reilly	20a 2r 37p	Rathmichael	
William Turbett	94a 3r 14p	Rathmichael	Rathmichael House
William Turbett	99a 3r 5p	Shankill	Mullinastill House
James C. Dodwell	30a 0r 19p	Shankill	Shankill House
Ebenezer Beggs	6a 1r 18p	Shankill	Shanganagh Cottage
James C. Dodwell	49a	Shankill	Shankill Castle
P. McAneny	104a 0r 0p	Shankill	

In the above table, Turbett is included twice as he held adjoining farms in the two townlands. The Valuation records have his name as the occupier of both houses, though Joseph Mills places Sam Turbett in Rathmichael House.[78] The land occupied by McAneny has been aggregated from a number of smaller plots for this table. Beggs had only a small area of land, but it was a significant house, with a gate-lodge. Joseph Mills stated that Henry Greville was evicted from Shankill Castle in Sir Charles' time;[79] this is not correct, however, as Greville had gone by 1856, before Sir Charles inherited the property;[80] it is possible that he was evicted by Sir Compton Domvile.

After Felix Hughes' negotiations, the tenants held on to most of his land: His original holding had included a substantial amount of mountain land and this, amounting to 42 acres, was handed back to Sir Charles Domvile, while Hughes continued to hold 54 acres on lower ground through to the late 1870s.[81] William Turbett fared less well. He had refused to renew his tenancy at what Domvile's solicitor considered 'an adequate rent;'[82] after many months of haggling agreement was not reached and William Turbett quit the farm';[83] with him went his subtenants, including Thomas Greene, Catherine Higgins, John Norton and George Walker at Mullinastill and an unidentified labourer at Rathmichael.[84] James Crofton Dodwell and Ebenezer Beggs also received

Sir Charles Domvile's attention, though Beggs remained in his house, now known as Ferndale, until his death a few years later. James C. Dodwell and his family had to fight a court case to hold on to their property. Dodwell's father-in-law, Jasper Fowler, built Shankill House, in the late 1820s, and by 1855 it was in Dodwell's possession.[85] In about 1856 he also acquired Shankill Castle, with 49 acres, and it seems likely that he occupied Shankill Castle while members of the family remained in Shankill House.[86] In December 1857 the validity of the lease under which the Fowler family was holding Shankill House was questioned by Sir Charles and his solicitor.[87] Domvile took a case against Anne Isabella Fowler and members of her family in 1858 in an attempt to have them evicted, but they remained in possession.[88] Shankill House and Shankill Castle remained in the occupation of James C. Dodwell until his death in the 1880s, following which they were both held by his son-in-law, John S. Murray.[89] The remaining two names on the list of larger tenants were James Dolan and Michael Reilly, who held adjoining plots on the hillside at Rathmichael. Sir Charles seems to have favoured Reilly, as no attempt seems to have been made to remove him from his land. On the contrary, in 1862 Domvile issued instructions to his solicitor to serve notice to quit 'on all tenants of Shankill except Reilly & Sigsworth.'[90] Dolan, however, was evicted. In December 1861 a writ was issued against him, apparently for failure to pay his rent, and the matter was put in the hands of the sheriff.[91] The following September Dolan was described as 'a weekly tenant',[92] but notice to quit was again served in December 1862.[93] This time James Dolan left his holding, and it was given over to Michael Reilly.[94]

A substantial number of holdings in Shankill and Rathmichael were smaller than those held by James Dolan and Michael Reilly. Once the matters of Toole's land and the more substantial tenancies had been addressed, Domvile turned his attention to the smallholdings. During the summer of 1862 he changed the terms under which tenants held their land so that rent was payable quarterly instead of every six months. In addition, the period of notice required was reduced from six months to one month. The editorial in an unidentified newspaper commented at the time:

The latest sample of model landlordism

> One lord paramount in [the Shanganagh] region is a certain Sir Charles Domvile ... This man's name has been paraded so much latterly at the heads of advertisements about pious bazaars, charity sermons, and what more besides, that we were half inclined to look upon him as a sort of beneficial angel.
>
> But the proceedings in the *Nisi Prius* court, last Saturday, ... awakened us from our pleasant dream. This benevolent baronet ... has, it seems, introduced into Irish landlordism a patent improvement utterly

unknown before. To evict, after a six months notice, a tenant who was willing to pay his rent, has been hitherto considered a coarse, harsh and brutal thing by some soft-hearted people. But on this custom [Domvile] has introduced an improvement which will open their eyes a little. He has compelled his tenants *to accept a month's notice alone* ... The man's own agent swore that [Sir Charles] compelled the tenants to accept an agreement by which they can be flung out of their holdings at one single month's notice ... In the very heart of the town where you have neither crop nor tillage, nor a shilling's expenditure, the landlord of your house must give you a half-year's notice.[95]

Yearly tenancies were common, and were assumed by the courts to exist whenever there was a doubt as to the nature of the tenancy.[96] In these cases a landlord could terminate a tenancy, but six months' notice was required.[97] A tenancy at will, on the other hand, could be ended at any moment by demand of possession without previous notice.[98] What Domvile appears to have been introducing here was a tenancy at will, but with a month's notice rather than no notice at all, a hybrid between tenancy at will and yearly tenancy. As will be discussed below, this type of tenancy was not to find favour in court.

Joseph Mills claimed that the rent was increased, stating that Sir Charles held an agricultural show at Santry for his tenants of Santry and Shankill:

> the Santry men only put in the poorest of their produce, while the foolish Shankill people, to win the prize, borrowed, and in some cases stole better turnips and mangolds than they were able to raise themselves, with the result that Sir Charles decided that the land that could produce such fine crops could pay a good deal more rent ...[99]

Whatever the accuracy of this story, the rents payable by at least some of the tenants at Shankill was increased by 50 per cent.[100] It is difficult to quantify the increases and the numbers of tenants affected, as many of the dozen or so whose rent went up were those who were taking on additional land at the time, such as Ralph Sigsworth, Micheal Kearns and Pat Byrne, and some of the increase may represent changes to the quantity of land held. In some cases the rent was increased when the land was allocated to a new tenant. Amongst those with the largest increases were Benjamin Tilly whose rent went up by 50 per cent, and Domvile's own brother William, whose rent for about 18 acres near Shankill Castle was more than doubled.

At this point Sir Charles became aware that some of the tenants of smallholdings had begun to sink sand pits and to quarry building stones which were then carried off and sold.[101] The mineral rights of the property had never been granted to the Domviles, and the head landlord had leased them to the Mining Company of Ireland as recently as 1858.[102] When Sir Charles

5 John Brack's house at Shankill.

sought legal opinion on the issue of tenants removing sand and stones, he also raised the matter of their tenancies. He found that the tenants had held their holdings from year to year in his father's time, but that Sir Charles had never recognized the tenancies. Counsel was requested to consider what proceedings should be taken to recover possession from the cottiers as Sir Charles 'finds it expedient to remove some tenants of this class'.[103] In August 1862 Sir Charles Domvile discovered that one of the tenants at Rathmichael, John Brack, had removed two cartloads of stone, and Domvile instructed his solicitor to take proceedings against him and to warn others – Brack's house is shown in figure 5.[104] On the same day, Domvile's solicitor, Randle Peyton, informed him that his agents, Stewarts and Kincaid, were prepared to give their reasons as to why they thought it inadvisable to eject 15 tenants from Shankill.[105]

At this stage, Sir Charles' agent at Shankill received a threatening letter. Threatening letters made up the largest category of agrarian outrage recorded by the constabulary at this period. They usually contained warnings or threats against the landlord or agent or, indeed, against other tenants, and were written either anonymously or under a pseudonym.[106] They were taken seriously and Domvile reacted immediately, directing his solicitor to have notices to quit served on 58 tenants at Shankill and Rathmichael with the least possible delay[107] Peyton contacted the land agents for the list, but Sir

Implementation 31

Charles was impatient and wanted to know how soon the 58 tenants could be legally dispossessed.[108] Land agent James Kincaid responded that there had been an agreement that no tenants of Shankill would be served until the following month.[109] Sir Charles was having none of this, however, and demanded that the notices to quit be ready for his signature the following day.[110] The notices were prepared, but not all were followed through and on 28 August Sir Charles signed the notices for 22 tenants.[111]

In his endeavour to establish the identity of the sender of the threatening letter Sir Charles Domvile engaged the services of a London detective agency.[112] The suggestion emerged that the writer of the letter had been John Brack. Sir Charles asked the Bank of Ireland to have one of its experts on handwriting examine the letter, and the secretary of the mining company, where Brack may have worked, was asked to inspect any documents which they may have had in Brack's handwriting.[113] Official channels were also engaged, though the chief secretary's office did not receive this notification until 29 October, more than two months after the letter was received.[114] The case was referred by the under secretary to a detective in the Metropolitan Police.[115] Following the issue of notices to quit an anonymous letter was received by the local newspaper, the *Bray Gazette*, denying the existence of a threatening letter:

> To the Editor of the *Bray Gazette*
>
> Sir, if you refer to — in your notice of agrarian outrages he or his agent has been served with no threatening letter in this neighbourhood, notwithstanding notice of eviction served on 25 or 30 tenants at —, most honest, peaceful tenants in the world, after raising their rent 50 per cent, making them pay quarterly. The less you pollute your columns with his name the better.
>
> A Constant Reader

Despite all his endeavours, Sir Charles was unable to prove Brack's authorship and could take no further action than to serve notice to quit along with the other tenants.

In tandem with his action at Shankill, Domvile instigated moves against tenants on the lands in Roscommon which he had inherited from his aunts. The parallels between Shankill and Roscommon grew when Domvile's agent in Roscommon, Mr Garnett, received a threatening letter. In this instance, however, the alleged perpetrator was caught. As a contemporary newspaper account described it:

> A constabulary force of thirty men attended Mr Garnett and the sub-sheriff on Thursday last to execute those long-pending ejectments at the

suit of Sir Charles Domvile ... [who] expressed his determination to eject the people living in the 'suspected' portion of his property if the offender was not discovered – why, Lord Derby only threatened in the event of a murder to carry out such an intention, but his better nature subsequently recoiled from the odium of such an act ... Yet it is well for the landlord and for the tenants that such an ordeal is not in store for either of them. It is deplorable to hear a fellow mortal ... pledge himself to depopulate the countryside because the writer of a threatening letter is not discovered, of which nine tenths of the sufferers can possibly know nothing.[116]

In mid-September the tenants at Shankill attempted to render the notices to quit void by accepting the increase in rent and paying it, but this placated neither James Kincaid nor Sir Charles, who directed Randle Peyton to serve notices to quit on all tenants of Shankill, except two. The exceptions were Ralph Sigsworth at Shankill and Michael Reilly at Rathmichael, who were to receive possession of the lands which had been cleared of tenants.[117]

The state of affairs at Shankill by mid-September 1862 was summarized in a report prepared for Sir Charles:

> In accordance with the terms of agreement under which the Shankill tenants hold ... Sir Charles has lately caused a month's notice to quit to be served, terminable on 29th September 1862. The actual intention of Sir Charles is not to evict all the tenants but attain a position by which he may legally carry out certain contemplated improvements by enlarging the holdings and diminishing the number of occupiers and erecting new fences ... in lieu of unsightly and irregular ditches ...
>
> Sir Charles, who is tenant for life, only intends to procure the erection of said fences by such means as may entitle him to charge the incidental expenses upon the inheritance ...[118]

This report contains the essential clue to the reasoning behind Sir Charles' decision to evict the smallholders at Shankill, and it is notable that it makes no mention of a threatening letter. The writer was being somewhat disingenuous, though, as meaningful consolidation would necessarily require the removal of the majority of the occupiers of the land. The statement that Sir Charles was tenant for life, and intended to erect fences 'by such means as may entitle him to charge ... expenses upon the inheritance' is critical. On 30 August, Randle Peyton had attended at the Board of Works on behalf of Sir Charles to enquire about loans for farm buildings and had discovered that these were not available where the valuation on the farms was less than £100.[119] It is no coincidence that three days later Peyton was asked to establish which tenants could produce £100, though the reason given was that Domvile 'wanted a class of men on the hill'.[120]

On 26 September 1862, with the date of the evictions looming, Sir Charles announced that he would be willing to leave any tenant in possession of their property as a caretaker if he or she gave up possession quietly though he would eject anyone immediately who should refuse to give up possession.[121] After eviction day had passed, Randle Peyton informed Domvile that the small tenants at Shankill would become caretakers on getting their crops, paying their rents up to 29 September, but the next day he had a response from Sir Charles stating that he would not allow any of the Shankill tenants to remain.[122] Peyton replied that all tenants who had been served notice in August, except four, had declined to give up their holdings unless they were allowed their crops and it appears that it was the issue of the crops that led to the impasse.[123] However, it was not to remain an impasse for long, as Domvile took proceedings for ejectment, even though the tenants had paid up their rent and refused to move.[124] Notices to quit, due to expire on 29 November, were prepared in relation to the tenants who still refused to relinquish their holdings.[125] Many of the tenants were evicted in December, and on 20 December Phineas Riall recorded that he went up to Shankill and found 'a desolate prospect, the hill on fire and all the cabins unroofed.'[126]

Court proceedings were brought against the eleven tenants who still held out and the hearing took place at the county court at Kilmainham on 9 January 1863;[127] the tenants were Thomas Doyle, Darby Doyle, William Everard, Charles Kearney, Laurence Lawless and Christopher Farrell of Shankill, and George Byrne, John Brack, John Confrey, James Cassidy and John Hogarty of Rathmichael. Brack, Cassidy and Hogarty were the only three to contest the case, the rest having allowed judgment to go by default.[128] Following the case, John Hogarty was gone from his holding relatively swiftly, while James Cassidy and John Brack remained in possession.[129] Cassidy continued to occupy his holding for more than three years but was ejected in 1866.[130] John Brack, however, managed to survive three cases against him in court. On the third occasion, in March 1864 Sir Charles Domvile introduced a new strategy for discouraging tenants from challenging his attempts to remove them from their holdings: he invoked the Landlord and Tenant Act 1860 which contained a provision that, where a case was taken for ejectment, the court could insist that the tenant give security before being permitted to present a defence.[131] Since inheriting the estate, Sir Charles had taken a high-handed attitude to his smaller tenancies at Shankill, with many of the tenants never receiving a new tenancy. Others, such as John Brack, had a new agreement, which he had signed but which Sir Charles had not, and, because of this, the three judges refused to grant Domvile's plea. Mr Justice Hayes felt that the agreement under which Brack held the property was not a proper agreement between two parties. He then went on to make strong comments about the nature of the agreement, its mere one-month notice and its inconsistency as to whether it was a yearly, quarterly or monthly tenancy, going so far to say that the terms were repugnant and that he was not disposed to give encouragement to such agreements. The chief justice held similar views, and stressed that this provision of that act was so onerous that it should only be used in exceptional circumstances.[132]

The *Irishman* reported the story in a more emotive vein:

Sir Charles Domvile again

There is something encouraging, as well as much that is revolting, in the report of a proceeding in the Queen's Bench, which will be found elsewhere in our columns. The notorious SIR CHARLES DOMVILE brought in that action of ejectment against a man named JOHN BRACKEN (*sic*), having served on him, on November last with a notice to quit and deliver up his house in one month from that day – that is ON CHRISTMAS DAY. Not satisfied with this act of unparalleled brutality, he comes before the Court with a motion for the purpose of preventing the wretched man, who has the misfortune to be his tenant, from taking defence until he should give sufficient security for the payment of all costs and damages that might be recovered against him, if defeated.[133]

Brack was usually late in his rent payments, and when he reached a full year's rent unpaid in September 1866 proceedings for ejectment were taken against him. He managed to remain in possession even though he did not clear the arrears for some months. Legal proceedings were threatened in 1871 due to arrears; however, he managed to remain in possession once again.[134] He and his family remained on the property into the 21st century. Joseph Mills recorded that John (Jack) Brack had fought Sir Charles in law and won, 'because the back of his house was in the mearing ditch which divided Sir Charles's land from' Ballycorus.[135] This may explain Brack's record in resisting eviction when so many others failed. His house was certainly built off the townland boundary between Rathmichael and Ballycorus.[136] Mills implied that because of this the house was partly in one townland and partly in the other and the courts would not grant possession to Domvile because not all of the house was on Domvile's property. At any rate, it is ironic that one of the few tenants to survive the evictions was seemingly the one who triggered the initial move against the smallholders, and may have been the writer of the letter which brought the action to a higher level.

3. Success or failure?

In June 1861, with the surrender of Toole's leases almost complete, Sir Charles Domvile advertised building ground for sale in the pages of the *Bray Gazette*:

Building sites at Shankhill [sic] near Bray

Shankhill, the property of Sir Charles Domvile, Bart., is situated half-a-mile from the sea, midway between Killiney and Bray, and contains 1,600 acres, with an undulating surface, forming hills and valleys, ranging from 100 feet to 1,000 feet above sea level. The entire lands have been laid out by Mr Fraser, Landscape Gardener, on a comprehensive and uniform plan for BUILDING PLOTS, containing from 2 to 12 acres each, and are so arranged that the plantations and buildings now and hereafter existing, cannot shut out the magnificent views of the sea, headlands and mountains, with which the neighbourhood

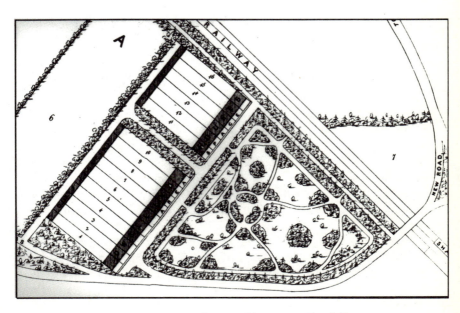

6 Proposed site of terraced houses at Shankill.
Source: National Library of Ireland, map reference 16 G 42 (21)

abounds. The hill-sides and valleys are planted, new lines of roads and beautiful drives are being formed ... On these lands, convenient to the building sites, are several quarries of granite and trap-rock, and delicious spring water is generally found near the surface. The Railway Station, 9 miles from Dublin and 2½ from Bray, is distant from some sites only three minutes walk. Long leases can be given. Full particulars may be learned from Messrs STEWARTS and KINCAID, Agents, 6, Leinster Street, or R. PEYTON, Solicitor, 83 Middle Abbey Street, Dublin. [1]

Figure 6 shows a detail of the map produced at this time to set out the building plots. The words 'new road' are at the point where Stonebridge Road leaves the Dublin Road at Shankill, with the plot marked '7' being the present site of Rathmichael Parish National School. A total of 11 sites for villas were shown, in addition to the 16 terrace plots and the small park. This land was developed in the late 19th century to provide Falls Road.

This advertisement appeared each week in the *Bray Gazette* until mid-July, after which a reduced version appeared for the following month. Once he had possession of Charles Toole's lands Sir Charles set about re-letting the property to tenants. Sir Charles found just one builder willing to take a building lease on a significant portion of the property. James Douglass, the builder who was constructing the parish church, had already taken on a lease of a small plot of land adjacent to Shankill railway station, formerly part of the holding of Sarah Doyle, who had been evicted.[2] He now took on nearly 80 acres, including the plots formerly occupied by the Revd Hackett at Lordello, Dr. Biggar at Ellerslie, Mrs Morgan at Springmount, Miss Gernon at Aughmore, the lands of Mrs Byrne and Mrs Burke and the former site of Shankill View. Where there was a substantial house on the lands the valuation was changed to include the house separately from most of its lands, implying that the land was to be developed separately.[3] The only mentions in Randle Peyton's day book relating to these plots are unspecific, such as 'Mr Douglass's proposition to take three-acre field at Shankill for building at rate of £8 per statute acre' and 'Mr Douglass ... expressed desire to take building lot at Shankill'.[4] However, deeds were executed, but not registered, including one in December 1863 which included Lordello, granted to James Douglass and his son Francis.[5] This accords with the rentals of Shankill, which include Douglass for the first time in March 1864.[6]

The Douglasses began to build on their land holdings at Shankill, but only on a very small scale. On Sarah Doyle's former plot close to the railway station they began the construction of two houses and at Lordello they added to the outbuildings.[7] Within a year of taking on this building land, however, the Douglasses were in financial trouble and threatened with bankruptcy.[8] They did not lose the Shankill property at this stage, however, though they were in danger of eviction through violation of the terms of their leases. In December

1864, Domvile considered that they had broken up ancient pasture, and in the same month they took a lawsuit against him for entering their land at Ellerslie and taking five tons of turnips in lieu of money they owed.[9] A month later, in January 1865, Sir Charles' solicitor advised him that he would succeed in getting an injunction against the Douglasses for allegedly destroying and removing shrubs from their holdings at Shankill in contravention of their leases.[10] A year later James and Francis Douglass were still in financial difficulties and the question of surrendering their leases at Shankill arose.[11] Domvile's solicitor, W.J. Cooper, met with the Douglasses and their solicitor to discuss the arrears of rent, which extended to six months' arrears on Springmount and a three-acre plot, and one and a half year's rent on Ellerslie.[12] The extent of their difficulties became apparent when Cooper was informed that the Douglasses had pawned three of their leases.[13]

The negotiations towards the surrender of the six leases held by the Douglasses continued through March and April 1866, with an element of urgency attaching to the Ellerslie lease as Domvile's agents had a new tenant ready to take on the property.[14] The surrender of the land at Lordello in the courts was delayed as it was found that there was not quite a year's rent overdue.[15] In April 1866, Ellerslie was surrendered.[16] Towards the beginning of June, the leases were surrendered on Springmount and two other plots of land.[17] Domvile had to wait until January for Lordello and February for the plot near the station.[18] In the meantime, the only houses that the Douglasses had commenced at Shankill were demolished while the negotiations were under way for surrender of the leases. Sir Charles' agent, Mr Kincaid, informed him that the Douglasses were about to remove a house on a small plot near the station and that he intended to prevent the removal but he was too late.[19] The valuation inspector noted in March 1866 that one of the houses was 'badly finished and to be taken down', while the other remained for a time, became dilapidated and was noted in March 1869 as 'of no use, no windows or doors, going into dilapidation' and it was subsequently demolished.[20]

Apart from the Douglasses, Domvile did not attract the potential builders of villas with the sole exception of Ballybride, as noted below. George Perrin, who was a solicitor rather than a builder, leased the properties at Chantilly and Silvermount, but did not build new villas on the lands. The valuation of the house at Chantilly actually fell as the amount of land attached to the house was reduced, and the valuation inspector noted that 'part of the buildings down and too many offices for the land.'[21] At Silvermount (now Sylvan Mount), the valuer reduced the valuation on the house dramatically from £23 10s. to £10, noting that 'buildings much out of repair. Mr Perrin says he will take them down, Feb. 1865.'[22] Two years later, when the valuer noted that a new tenant was in occupation, the valuation increased to £15, with the note that the house was improved.[23] Just one other house at Shankill was improved significantly at this time.[24] James C. Dodwell, as has been noted, had leased

Shankill Castle shortly before Sir Charles inherited the estate, and he made significant additions to the outbuildings, resulting in an increase in the valuation from £22 to £37.[25]

As Benjamin Tilly's objection to the terms of the lease shows, Sir Charles was not merely accepting the surrender of a lease and then renegotiating it at a higher rent, he was also introducing new conditions. This had begun relatively early, in November 1857, when he asked his solicitor to consider his rights to have his servants enter any leasehold premises to ascertain whether the covenants of the lease were being observed.[26] In March 1861, Sir Charles began to introduce significant changes to the leases which he was offering, proposing that they should contain a clause forbidding any building except with his approval.[27] Two weeks later he wanted clauses that stipulated that all rents must be paid within two months and that there be no subletting without his sanction.[28] A week after that he decided that, despite an earlier decision, he would not after all allow any grazing at Shankill, but would allow meadow for hay making.[29] In July he gave his solicitor instructions relating to clauses regarding rights of entry for his game keeper.[30] In December he decided that he would charge his tenants the full cost of the poor rates, provided he was legally permitted to do so, and he directed his solicitor in relation to 'additional clauses to be inserted into leases', the nature of which Peyton did not record.[31] Three days later, in response to a problem which occurred on his lands at Coolock, he asked that future leases should include a provision that forbade the removal of hedges.[32] The following July an amended draft building lease was prepared for release to anyone enquiring about building ground.[33] Finally, in August 1862, Domvile gave directions that whenever he received a loan under the land acts for the improvement of holdings the interest on any money paid out should be paid by the tenant.[34] While the exact nature of these changes over time is uncertain, it would appear that the covenants in Domvile's leases were becoming onerous, and the piecemeal way in which he was making these additions suggests that he was not thinking the issue through in a systematic way.

That these clauses were unusually burdensome is suggested by Tilly's preference to move house rather than accept the terms, even though this had been the family home for more than thirty years. His father, Robert Tilly, had taken a lease in 1828, and had built the house called Chantilly, conveying the lands to Benjamin Tilly in 1849.[35] One single incident proves little, but this incident was not isolated. Late in 1861 a certain Mr Stanley, the occupier of a house in Shanganagh townland, put forward a proposal for a tract of land in Shankill.[36] On seeing the proposed lease, Stanley raised objections and wished to back out of negotiations.[37] Sir Charles refused to accept the advice of his solicitor that he could not compel Stanley to take the lease and instructed him that he would not vary the terms of the proposed lease and that he would seek an order for specific performance from Stanley.[38]

At the same time, negotiations were under way with Charles Toole who wished to take a building lease on part of the lands he had formerly held, but this came to nothing.[39] Also at this time negotiations with a potential lessee of the property known as Ballybride failed. The house at Ballybride had been vacant at the time it was surrendered by Charles Toole in July 1861, and it was not until December that a potential lessee was found in James Mackey, proprietor of Mackey's Seeds, and son of Stephen Mackey, former partner of the Toole family.[40] This deal fell through, the house was re-advertised, and six months later a potential occupier was found in G.H. Hackett.[41] Negotiations commenced, but by 8 August, Hackett announced that he objected to the draft lease and by 20 August it was decided to readvertize the house as negotiations with Hackett had broken off.[42] After trying for a year to find an occupier for Ballybride, and having lost one potential lessee, Sir Charles would not soften his approach to the leases sufficiently to dispose of the property. It was two and a half years before another potential lessee emerged, in Charles Bennett who was the auctioneer who had been advertising the property.[43] The lease was signed in November 1865 and Bennett immediately set about building a new house.[44] This was a substantial house, now known as Cornerstown House, and was given a valuation of £45, higher than any other house on the Shankill estate.[45] In June 1869 Charles Bennett leased the property to a subtenant for £1,700.[46]

Sir Charles did not exclude his brother, William C. Domvile, from his actions. He took him to court over their aunt's will,[47] and in September 1862 served notice to quit on him in relation to land he occupied at Shankill.[48] A few weeks later William served notice on Sir Charles' tenants in Roscommon, telling them not to pay rent to Sir Charles.[49] Subsequently, following the death of their sister Emily in 1864, Sir Charles's solicitor advised him not to go to litigation over her estate. Emily Domvile had been left £35,000 by her father with the proviso that on her death two fourths of it would go to William C. Domvile and the other fourths would go to her sisters Lady Winnington and Madame de Billa.[50] Domvile disregarded his solicitor and sued his brother again. In the meantime, William Domvile quit the 18 acres he held near Shankill Castle.[51]

Sir Charles intended to improve agricultural holdings through the removal of unsightly fences and providing new ones.[52] In Rathmichael townland, though, the extent of these works was less than impressive. The estate maps produced in the mid-1850s show field boundaries at the time of Sir Charles's inheritance of the estate.[53] The second edition Ordnance Survey six-inch map was published in 1871 in the immediate aftermath of Sir Charles' changes of the 1860s.[54] Comparison of these two maps shows that a total of 14 per cent of the fences was removed in Rathmichael, and a similar amount of new fences provided. Much of this was due to the construction of two roads through the townland, and if these are eliminated from the equation there was a nett reduction of 7 per cent in the amount of fences in the townland.[55] By contrast, in Ticknick townland which adjoined Rathmichael to the north, in the same period nearly 40 per cent of field boundaries were removed, and after the construction of new boundaries there was a nett reduction of 15 per cent. The corresponding changes in Shankill townland are less straightforward to assess, due to the mix of land with the bigger houses, though a great deal may be seen from visual inspection of the Ordnance Survey maps of 1843 and 1871. The removal or reorganization of field boundaries took place in Shankill in very limited areas. The smaller farm holdings in Shankill townland were grouped into four main areas, with the remainder of the land being held by the gentry or larger farmers, or as mountain land. The northernmost group lay along the Bride's Glen, along the valley slopes where the valley was narrow and the gradients steep. In the main these were taken over by Sir Charles for planting, as seen above. The second group was the small cluster of holdings in the vicinity of Shankill Castle, at the junction of Ferndale Road, Lordello Road and Quarry Road. Most of these holdings went in the clearance of the lands held by Charles Toole. A third, small, group lay on the western edge of the townland on the far side of the hill and they mostly disappeared, with the field boundaries remaining. The final, and largest, group was spread along Quarry Road as it climbed from Shankill Castle to the hillside and the iron shooting lodge towards the south-west and here the most dramatic changes to field boundaries occurred, with the removal of the majority of the landholders and the consolidation of their fields into larger farms. Only one significant new fence was laid out, orientated so close to east-west and ignoring the natural lie of the land so completely that it must have been set down on paper in an office somewhere other than Shankill. This part of the estate represents the most successful part of Domvile's plan to consolidate holdings and set out more efficient field systems and in so doing the number of families living in this section of Shankill was reduced from twenty-two to seven.

In 1857 there were 47 land-holding tenants living in Shankill townland, with an average of 15.2 acres; by 1871 this had risen to 27.8 acres. If the houses of the gentry are removed from the equation, the average farm size was just 8.4 acres, increasing to 33.8 acres in 1871. As with Rathmichael, these figures exclude land held by someone not living in the townland. The farm holdings in Shankill in 1871 occupied less than a third of the townland, with the balance taken up with land attached to houses of the gentry, or held by non-residents. In addition, Sir Charles Domvile himself held over 300 acres, the bulk of which was hillside suitable only for rough grazing, with a further 60 acres held for development purposes. Sir Charles did not let this land go idle, but kept his own cattle on part of the property.[56]

As well as these actual improvements to the Shankill estate others were envisaged, but not completed. For instance, in July 1863 Richard A. Gray, surveyor, produced a specification for Sir Charles Domvile for a farm dwelling

Success or failure?

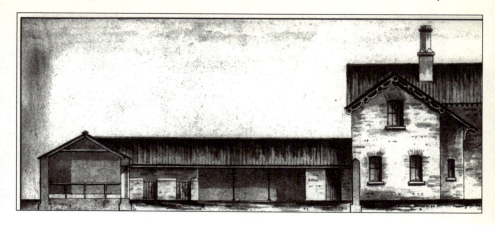

7 Proposal for farm house at Shankill.
Source: National Library of Ireland drawing reference AD 2455

and offices at Shankill.[57] This was to be a substantial farm house built in stone with brick surrounds to the doors and windows. Its out-offices were to include a piggery, young cattle house, potato store, barn, cart shed, stable and dairy. Plans and elevations for the farm house were drawn up by Sandham Symes as shown in figure 7. Symes was the architect who was working for Sir Charles at Santry House, but the proposed farm house at Shankill never built.[58]

Sir Charles' iron shooting lodge ran into problems even before it was finished. In the case taken against Domvile in April 1863, the builder James Douglass sought payment of £772 for the erection of a coach house 22 ft by 19 ft. Domvile, however, thought it 'more likely that he mentioned twenty-four feet by nine as the former would be unreasonably and needlessly large.' His defence was undermined by the revelation that his bailiff at Shankill, Isaac Webster, had seen the site several times during construction and, seemingly, had never raised the dimensions as an issue.[59] For reasons unknown, the Iron Lodge did not last long. The valuation records in February 1868, noted 'Iron house taken down', and most of the land was in the hands of Peter Whelan.[60] The house was shown on the second edition Ordnance Survey six-inch sheet, however, though this claims to have been revised in 1871.[61] It may well be that Sir Charles had been ahead of his time in using iron in a building for his own occupation. It is unlikely that insulation methods had been fully developed and occupation during the summer season could have been unbearable in hot weather. Noise insulation would have been as bad, and the noise of rain would have carried throughout the building. Not long after Sir Charles had built his iron lodge a meeting of the Royal Institute of British

Architects discussed the pros and cons of iron buildings. One of the chief problems identified was rust, and one delegate, William White, thought that rusting would preclude its use for outside walls unless they were enamelled, and he spoke 'with regard to the changes of atmosphere and temperature which might render a building untenable for domestic purposes'.[62] It is possible that Sir Charles and Lady Domvile discovered these disadvantages for themselves and simply stopped using the lodge. Joseph Mills had this to say: 'Sir Charles built his iron ball-proof house ... a very short time after his marriage had it pulled down and the iron sold. A man presumably from Dublin bought it and stored it in Peter Kearney's, but forgot to come for it'.[63] The idea of the lodge being ball-proof is fanciful. Conventional masonry buildings are ball-proof, if such a building is required. Sheet iron would have to be thicker than conventional corrugated iron to be ball-proof.

In the 1860s the Rathdown board of guardians proposed a new public cemetery to serve its area and invited tenders, and Sir Charles Domvile submitted a tender offering three to four acres at Shankill at £10 per acre in perpetuity.[64] The presence of a cemetery would not have been helpful in finding takers for villa sites and would have had no spin-off benefits for the estate. However, with the Rathdown union workhouse at Loughlinstown standing just outside the estate and its infirmary lying within the townland of Shankill, Sir Charles probably felt that a cemetery adjoining the workhouse would do no harm to the letting potential of the rest of his estate. As it happened he was unsuccessful in his bid, the board of guardians opting for a more centrally-placed site at Dean's Grange, at £200 plus a rent of £6 per acre.[65]

It had been part of Sir Charles Domvile's plan for his Shankill estate that new roads would be provided to open up the lands for development. This process had begun in his father's time when Sir Compton Domvile had provided Puck's Castle Lane along the hillside and Stonebridge Road leading westwards from Shankill railway station. Sir Compton had other plans for roads,[66] including one leading from the western end of Stonebridge Road up the hillside to meet Puck's Castle Lane and another from Stonebridge Road just west of the railway line heading south and west to join up with Lordello Road which it would have realigned, leading to the old town of Shankill and thence up the hillside. These two roads were never built, but when combined with the two that Sir Compton did manage to lay out they would have opened up the land very successfully for development. James Fraser's report had suggested different road layouts, but none of his proposed roads was built.

The only new road to be built on the Shankill estate during Sir Charles Domvile's time was erected by the grand jury, which was the county authority responsible for the construction and maintenance of roads and bridges. The advent of the railway had made the Shankill area more accessible and the Mining Company of Ireland was one of the beneficiaries. This company brought lead ore to its works at Ballycorus from its mines in Wicklow, in addition to bringing coal for the furnaces and delivering finished lead products to Dublin.[67] In April 1860 an application was made to the grand jury for a new road leading from Stonebridge Road to a point on Ballycorus Road which was at the top of the rise from the Bride's Glen. The justification was given in a report by Henry Brett, civil engineer, in which he stated that 'the Mining Company as well as the inhabitants of the district generally have to draw heavy loads of coal, lime and general commodities as well as to bring down the produce to the nearest markets and to the railway'.[68] Articles of agreement were signed for the making of the road in September 1860, the contractor being Richard Roberts, one of Sir Charles Domvile's tenants at Rathmichael.[69] While this road was ordered and paid for by the grand jury, seemingly to serve the mining company and the district in general, Sir Charles appears to have played an important part behind the scenes. His solicitor drafted an account of expenses laid out between May and October 1860 and which included various sums relating to the presentment to the grand jury:[70]

> Amount received from Mining Company toward expenses of Shankill new road presentment, £25
> Cash to C.J. Johnston towards cost of Shankill new road memorial £10 in addition to £20 recently
> Amount made for specification of Shankill new road
> Cash paid to Brett and Frith for their services in relation to Shankill new road £21
> Paid for fee on Jury in Shankill new road case £3 3s. 0d.

It might be relevant to note that the members of a grand jury were selected by the high sheriff and that in 1860 the high sheriff of Co. Dublin was Domvile himself.[71] Among those whom he had selected to serve on the grand jury for this year were James R. Stewart, one of the partners in Stewarts and Kincaid, his land agents; James C. Dodwell, one of his substantial tenants at Shankill; Charles Cobb, a personal friend and one of the trustees in his deed of settlement with his father; and Phineas Riall, his neighbouring landowner at Old Connaught and Shanganagh.[72] While this does not necessarily mean that this would be a 'packed' jury that would automatically favour using public money to improve Domvile's Shankill estate, the combination of circumstances invites suspicion.

By 1868 Domvile had spent just under £46,000 on the improvement of his estates at Shankill and Santry.[73] Just over £3,100 of this was spent on Shankill, far short of the £17,000 estimated in 1862 when counsel's opinion was sought on a possible second Domvile estate act.[74] Comparison of the spending at Shankill with that at Santry shows that the biggest expense at

Shankill was the provision of the parish church, for which Domvile paid the builder £2,180. Interestingly, a similar amount, £2,132, was paid for gilding ceilings at Santry House. A sum of £232 was spent on roads at Shankill, compared with £837 for making and improving roads in and about the demesne at Santry. The planting in accordance with James Fraser's recommendations at Shankill cost £524, while Domvile spent £1,706 on planting at Santry.[75] These figures suggest that the resources were overwhelmingly concentrated at Santry, and that the attempts to improve Shankill were cursory.

It has been noted above that one of the reasons behind Sir Charles Domvile's restructuring of his Shankill estate was to improve the rental income. This would be done in four ways. First, he would eliminate middlemen, most particularly by taking back the land held by Charles Toole. Secondly, he would let land on leases for the building of villas. Thirdly, he would consolidate farm holdings into larger, more efficient units. Fourthly, rents could be increased. At the time that he inherited the estate the total income from rents at Shankill was £1,023.[76] By 1871 this had risen to £1,370, a rise of 34 per cent.[77] Shankill was the only one of the seven divisions of the Domvile estates in Dublin city or county to show a significant increase between 1857 and 1871. However, the rent at Shankill fell in the early 1860s as a result of the number of holdings which produced no rent due to evictions, and a low was reached in September 1863, recovering thereafter. In fact, while detailed breakdowns are not available between 1857 and 1862, there was a very sharp fall between those years from £1,023 to £896 in March 1862, falling further to £699 in September 1863. Rents on the Santry lands also fell severely, only rising above their 1857 level permanently in the mid-1860s. The reason for this is outside the scope of this study and would warrant further investigation.

The figures hide a very significant factor in the rents of the Shankill estate. The surrender of Charles Toole's leases meant that the whole of the rent was now coming to Domvile. In May 1861 Charles Toole's income from rents had been £494, while his head rent paid to Domvile was £443, giving a net profit of about £50.[78] In addition, Toole held 92 acres which was unlet and which he valued at £6 per Irish acre, or £342 per annum. If this is factored into the equation, Domvile's rents on Shankill ought to have increased by £392 on the surrender of Toole's lands to a total of £1,412 per annum. However, in reality Shankill was only bringing in £1,370 by 1871. In fact Toole is more likely to have obtained £3 per acre from his land, this being the rent paid by Benjamin Tilly on the adjoining property. If this figure is taken, the combined rent of Toole's land and Domvile's would come to £1,246. In this case the increase to £1,370 by 1871 would represent 10 per cent increase in 14 years. While this is a greater increase than on Domvile's properties at Balrothery, Ballyfermot, Finglas and Dublin city where the rents remained static, it is a modest rise by standards of the period.[79] In an examination of eleven estates for which rental records survive, W.E. Vaughan found that, between 1857 and 1871, six of the eleven experienced rises greater than 10 per cent, four of them having rises of 18, 19, 22 and 23 per cent.[80] Moreover, these rent increases were based on little or no change in the use of the land. Given that Domvile had intended to increase the rentals through consolidation of holdings and sale of leases for the building of villas, the lack of increases in his rents at Shankill can only be deemed a failure.

At the time of his inheritance in 1857 Sir Charles Domvile had an income of £16,300 a year, rising to £19,000 when he inherited land in Roscommon from his mother's family. After paying allowances to family members, he was left with £16,700.[81] A further tract of land in Tipperary which he inherited from his uncle in 1862 brought him £5,000 on its sale in 1863. Despite his large income and his planned improvements, Sir Charles was in financial difficulties by the early 1860s. Throughout his adult life he borrowed money from others such as his brother William and his friend William Caldwell.[82] Even before inheriting the family property he had raised money by way of a mortgage on it. In October 1857, just a few months after inheriting the family estates, a judgement was awarded against him in the court of queen's bench for a debt of £2,000.[83] In the same month he began to raise mortgages on the estate, and within two years he had borrowed more than £30,000.[84] There followed a three-year gap in Sir Charles Domvile's borrowings and he resumed the practice in 1862 with further loans totally almost £20,000 from assurance companies and private individuals.[85] As part of his security for these loans, particularly the private ones, he frequently offered insurance policies on his own life and over the years he took out many such policies from a variety of companies.[86]

Despite these loans, in the 1860s Sir Charles was running into debt with a number of contractors and suppliers and these were frequently turned into mortgages. These included £2,985 owed to William Fry and Co., merchants of Westmoreland Street; merchant Thomas Synnott; nurseryman Charles Toole, formerly of Shankill; his own land agents Stewarts and Kincaid; and his solicitor Randle Peyton.[87] In some cases the creditors became impatient, or nervous, and took the debt to court to obtain a judgment that could be registered as a mortgage. This included two judgments by his own solicitor, Randle Peyton, who obtained judgments of £2,000 and £1,360 in January 1864.[88] Understandably, Randle Peyton ceased to act as Domvile's solicitor; his replacement was W.J. Cooper. Randle Peyton's accounts of work carried out for Sir Charles had included negotiations of leases, court cases, evictions and so forth and while these also figure in Cooper's accounts, they are almost totally swamped by the need to administer Sir Charles's debts.[89] The creditors included architect Thomas Deane, builder George Carolin and timber merchants John Martin & Co; others included painters, upholsterers and corn merchants.[90] A great deal of Cooper's time was spent meeting with creditors whose loans had fallen due and negotiating extensions of time, often having to accept higher interest rates, or a down payment before the delay would be agreed. One of the principal creditors was Domvile's land agents, Stewarts and Kincaid, who frequently gave Sir Charles advances on rents to be collected.[91] In January 1866 Stewart agreed to take a bill of sale for the effects at Santry Court, Sir Charles' house, 'for his own and Sir Charles's protection', implying that the house was in danger of a visit from the sheriff to distrain goods for debts not paid.[92] There had come a point when it was clear that Sir Charles Domvile's financial affairs needed a radical boost and his Roscommon estate was put up for sale through the Landed Estates Court in 1864. Once this was set in train Cooper's task became one of holding off the creditors until the money came through from the sale, but this took time and it was January 1866 before any money was paid.[93]

Even as the proceeds from the sale of Roscommon came through, Sir Charles was borrowing again, asking Stewarts and Kincaid to re-lend £1,600 which was being repaid to them.[94] A week later Sir Charles had Cooper approaching members of the family to explore the possibility of a loan of family trust funds, but this was not successful.[95] That matters were serious despite the Roscommon money is evident in the offer by Sir Charles' wife, Margaret, to assign her pin money, though this was merely a gesture, as her husband was tens of thousands of pounds in debt, while her pin money amounted to £300 a year.[96] Nevertheless, Lady Domvile produced a cheque for £35 some months later as her contribution to the crisis.[97]

As the financial difficulties deepened, the decision was made to reschedule the debts and the Guardian Fire and Life Assurance Company was approached with a view to taking out a large loan.[98] Meanwhile, W.J. Cooper had to get all of the creditors to hold off until the money came through, and he persuaded Sir Thomas Deane not to issue proceedings for his debt still outstanding on his fees for designing Rathmichael parish church.[99] The money came through towards the end of November, £12,500 initially, out of a total of £90,000 which had been approved by Guardian.[100] Over the next few days and weeks Cooper was paying off various debts and arranging for the holders of various mortgages to assign them to the company in order to recoup their loans.[101] This massive injection of funds temporarily satisfied the creditors but did not bring an end to Domvile's financial difficulties. No sooner had Guardian advanced the loan than Sir Charles was negotiating with Stewarts and Kincaid who granted him another loan for £5,000 and agreed not to register the mortgage until all of the paperwork was completed with Guardian – in other words to conceal the transaction so as not to cause a problem.[102]

Domvile felt that expenditure which would improve the family property in the long term should not have to come from his own personal income, but should be chargeable to the estate, and soon after obtaining the Domvile

Estate Act 1860 he began moves to obtain a second act to give him the power to do this. He estimated that his expenditure by the beginning of 1862 had exceeded £30,000, of which £20,000 was on improvements of a permanent and beneficial nature. He wished to use the estate act to charge £15,000 of this on the estate and a further £17,000 for the improvement of Shankill and Rathmichael 'by building houses thereon under the direction of two or more trustees to be named in the bill'.[103] Counsel's opinion was that he was unlikely to gain approval if the act was opposed by members of the family and this the idea was not pursued for a number of years.[104] Ultimately, however, Domvile set the procedures in train, and the Domvile Estate Act, 1868 was given royal assent on 31 July of that year.[105] The act did not grant powers to charge the sums which Domvile had sought initially; it limited the amount to be charged on the estate to £12,500 in total and this sum was charged against the Santry and Shankill estates.[106] The Domvile Estate Act 1868 and the various loans helped Domvile's financial position, but he continued to run up new debts and consolidated them into a large institutional loan in 1872, following which he ran up further debts, many of which were with Stewarts and Kincaid.[107] Almost inevitably, Sir Charles Domvile's inability to contain his finances ended in bankruptcy, perhaps the only surprise being that this did not happen sooner than 1876.[108]

Estimating the amount spent by Domvile on interest is also difficult, given the numbers of mortgages he held and the range of debts which stemmed from bills not paid on time and which were subject to interest payments. With the sale of the Roscommon estate, his nett income would have fallen to about £14,000. If the large loan of £90,000 was subject to interest at 7 per cent, the total interest payable would be £6,300 per annum, representing 45 per cent of his nett income. W.E. Vaughan, in his analysis of the debts of landlords as a proportion of the incomes of their estates, has concluded that it is extremely difficult to make any comparison. However, he found that interest payments varied from nothing to 39 per cent of rental income, with the average being about 17 per cent.[109] If the encumbrances on an estate exceeded half of the rental income, a creditor could petition for the sale of the estate in the encumbered estates court and by now this critical proportion would have been reached.[110] Vaughan found that is generally difficult or impossible to show the cause of landlord indebtedness. The provision of incomes for large numbers of relatives, extravagant lifestyles and political careers were three significant drains on the income of a landlord, but precisely which is not always simple to ascertain in any one case.[111]

How Sir Charles Domvile spent his income is unclear. Domvile's expenditure on his estates at Shankill and Santry in the period 1857 to 1868 amounted to just under £46,000. In the same period his rental income would have exceeded £200,000. While the outlay on his estate was less than a quarter of his rental income, the inclusion of other outgoings demonstrates

Domvile's poor financial position. His income had been £19,000 in 1857, and this had been decreased by £2,700 on the sale of the Roscommon estate, and increased by £1,200 with higher rents, leaving an income of £17,500. Averaged over the period to 1868 expenditure on the estate came to £4,000 per annum, and with £2,300 to his sister-in-law and his wife and about £6,000 a year in interest payments, his available income would have been reduced to £5,200. While this was a substantial income at the time, it was not a significant disposable income for a man of his position. Even the professional fees for his solicitor and his agents, Stewarts and Kincaid, must have come to a significant proportion of this sum. In the light of these figures it is conceivable that Domvile found himself in a vicious circle in which his interest payments left him with insufficient funds to support his lifestyle and forced him to borrow more in order to maintain his expected standards.

4. Consequences

In the 1860s Sir Charles Domvile had cleared the smaller tenants off their holdings at Shankill and Rathmichael, seeking to retain only those with the resources to become larger farmers. Between the census years of 1861 and 1871 the population of Rathmichael townland halved from 120 to 58, and the houses reduced from 18 to 9.[1] These figures mask the full extent of the fall, however, as Sir Charles had commenced his clearance in the 1850s shortly after inheriting the property.[2] At the time that he inherited the Shankill estate there were 23 houses in Rathmichael townland, whereas by 1871 only 10 farm holdings remained – a fall of about 57 per cent. Examination of the farm holdings at Shankill shows a pattern similar to that at Rathmichael. Between 1861 and 1871 the population of Shankill townland fell from 440 to 183, and the number of houses from 82 to 34.[3] Omitting the 15 houses of substance from the equation, in that they do not represent smallholdings, then the fall in the number of houses on smallholdings or without land would represent a drop from 67 to 19, a fall of some 72 per cent. In terms of what Domvile set out to achieve, this element of his plans for his Shankill estate appears at first sight to have been a success, with the average farm holding at Rathmichael increasing from 21.9 acres to 36.3 acres.[4] The average farm size should have been more like 50 acres, but the figure is reduced due to an increase in the amount of land held by tenants resident outside the townland, and because Sir Charles himself held some 80 acres, or 20 per cent of the townland.[5]

At the time of the succession of Sir Charles Domvile to the family property in 1857 there was a total of 97 tenants living in the two townlands of Shankill and Rathmichael. By 1871, only 10 of these houses were occupied by the same person or family.[6] It is not certain how many of the 87 occupiers who left the estate were evicted and how many left of their own accord. The papers of the Domvile estate, including the account books of Randle Peyton and W.J. Cooper, do not spell out the precise details of the evictions, or even when eviction proceedings were set in train. The outcome of such proceedings need not necessarily have been eviction but could be renegotiation of the terms under which the land was held rather than final ejectment from the holding. The pamphlet by Joseph Mills identifies about 80 householders who left the estate, but in many cases it is unclear as to whether they were evicted, died or merely moved on by choice.[7] In any case, the dividing line between eviction and voluntary moving is blurred as the terms under which new leases were offered could effectively push an occupier out just as effectively as if ejectment proceedings had been taken.

The vast majority of the evictions and other changes in occupancy on the Shankill estate occurred during the agricultural crisis of the early 1860s. Through Ireland as a whole evictions increased in the period from 1861, almost doubling to 1864, after which they fell again.[8] However, the evictions in Shankill appear not to have been connected with the agricultural crisis. The crisis was not as severe in the area around Shankill as it was in many places as the land was more productive and there was relative prosperity arising from the gentry living in the area. Sir Charles Domvile was not one to offer assistance to his tenants at a time of poor harvests in the way that many landlords did. His timing in raising the rents so significantly during an agricultural depression suggests a harsh approach, but his behaviour in Roscommon offers more direct evidence. In May 1862 the secretary of the Dysart Relief Committee of Roscommon wrote to Sir Charles requesting a contribution. He was so outraged by the response that he revealed it in a letter to the *Roscommon Messenger*. In this he quoted from Domvile's reply thus:

> I feel quite sure that whenever money is to be distributed in the county of Roscommon there will be recipients, but as I do not believe in the reports of unusual distress, nor condemn the poor house system, I must decline subscribing.[9]

The secretary added his own comments:

> The answer he has given is creditable to him neither as a landlord nor a Christian, and highly insulting not only to the committee, but to the entire Co. Roscommon. Sir Charles has numerous tenantry in this parish, the great majority of whom are in a wretched state of destitution. How could they be otherwise for rents have been raised this very year upwards of fifty per cent.

In the spring of 1862 the *Bray Gazette* recorded that there was no excessive distress in the Shankill and Bray area in the winter just passed.[10] Five weeks later, in an article on evictions on the Fitzwilliam and Domvile estates the paper hoped that 'property holders in our locality will bear in mind the distress among small farmers'.[11] In the following winter, the *Gazette* again addressed the issue:

> Whether undue distress exists or not in this district amongst the poor is just now an agitated question. We have taken some trouble to gain information on the subject and ... although the amount of distress usual in severe winters is present amongst us, still it is not excessive, not sufficient to stamp upon the neighbourhood the ban of poverty ... as may be seen in the reports of the state of our Union Workhouse, ...

there are but thirty-three inmates there in excess of the corresponding periods of other years ... We have, therefore, no doubt that it would be full to overflowing if great distress really existed. Further, we have ascertained that employment is abundant and wages quite up to average height.[12]

Reports such as this need to be read with care. However, there was a significant factor in place, at least by 1863, that would act, in effect, as a scheme of relief works. Dublin Corporation's scheme to utilize the water of the Vartry river at Roundwood in Wicklow to supply water to Dublin had got under way in the autumn of 1862, the foundation stone of its reservoir at Stillorgan being laid in November.[13] This necessitated the construction of a large dam, lake, water works and tunnel at Roundwood, twelve miles south of Shankill, a relief tank at Rathmichael, on the Domvile estate, and a reservoir at Stillorgan, six miles to the north.[14] The same issue of the *Bray Gazette* that had discounted the presence of distress in the district reported that 200 workmen were employed at Stillorgan reservoir, with vacancies for more, a considerable number were working at the Roundwood reservoir and, in addition, Lord Powerscourt was employing many labourers to construct his ornamental lake at Powerscourt demesne, three miles from Shankill.[15] Critically, these works also involved the laying of massive cast-iron pipes along a route which passed through the Domvile estate at Shankill and Rathmichael, the pipes weighing two tons each and requiring a massive amount of labour to excavate the trenches. The first of these pipes arrived from Britain at the beginning of March 1863 and work was soon under way along the route.[16]

If the availability of work cushioned the tenants of Shankill from distress, it could not provide alternative accommodation when eviction occurred. So what happened to more than 80 families which were relocated from the Shankill estate? Perhaps surprisingly, very few of them had to resort to admission to the workhouse at the time of eviction, though some residents of the Shankill estate were admitted to the workhouse some time later. Many of them were noted as having some ailment, and may have been admissions to the hospital, as workhouses could fulfil this function from 1862.[17] John McAneny was evicted from Shankill by Sir Charles Domvile in 1862, and in March 1864 his son was admitted to the workhouse as he was sick.[18] A Patrick Byrne of Shankill, aged 80 and described as a labourer, was admitted to the workhouse in August 1864 and died there two weeks later.[19] He may have been described as a labourer in order to get him admitted as Patrick Byrne held 22 acres of land from Domvile. He was not one of those who had been evicted, but was probably admitted solely because of the state of his health. After his death, his son Matthew Byrne was able to increase the area of the holding and the family remained on the property.[20] John Mason was one of the landless tenants of Andrew and Catherine Tracy on Charles Toole's land near Shankill Castle, and Domvile evicted him as he was an under-tenant.[21] He was sick when he was admitted to the workhouse in November 1865 and died within a few months.[22] His widow, Rose Mason, was brought to the workhouse by the police in a state of 'mental excitement', accompanied by three daughters aged five, seven and 16. This seems to have been a nervous breakdown, as she was later admitted to the Richmond Lunatic Asylum.[23] Joseph Mason, living at Rathmichael, was one of the first to be evicted possibly in July 1859 when he was admitted to the workhouse aged 77 and infirm.[24] There was an almost total absence of admissions to the workhouse in the period immediately following eviction. That almost all of those who were admitted were sick or injured demonstrates that eviction was not the immediate reason for people to enter the workhouse, but use of the medical facilities offered in the hospital. It was also possible to get assistance from the workhouse without admission through outdoor relief. In fact, between 1860 and 1867 only two people from Shankill received outdoor relief, neither of whom were householders and it is likely that they were farm servants living on the farmer's premises.[25]

In the story told by Joseph Mills of the evictions he described the village of Tillystown, referring to the

> field that Mr Ben. Tilly let to the evicted tenants of Sir Charles when that gentleman ordered them to hell or the sea. This field was divided into plots, and every man that took a plot was required to build a house on it ... [M]ost of us settled here.[26]

Benjamin Tilly's landholding ran across the townland boundary into Shanganagh which was not owned by the Domviles.[27] On 9 December 1862, Tilly granted leases of a number of quarter-acre plots along a roadway laid out on his Shanganagh property.[28] Tenants on the Shankill estate had been served notice to quit in the summer, a second set was served to take effect on 29 November and the clearance took place in the third week of December.[29] The granting of leases at Tillystown took place in the interval between the expiry of the notices to quit and the actual eviction. Eleven people who did not quit their holdings were taken to court in January 1863, but before the court date eight of these had quit. Of these, four took on land at Tillystown, namely William Everard, Christopher Farrell, Laurence Lawless and Charles Kearney, all from the Quarry Road area of Shankill.[30]

Those who were evicted from Shankill at the same time as taking a site at Tillystown were left with the problem of where to live while constructing a house on the new land. It seems likely that many of these remained in their original holdings as caretakers as Domvile had suggested originally. This is certainly how William Everard managed, though he ran into trouble, as reported in the *Bray Gazette*:

W. Everet [sic] a labouring man, before [the magistrates] at suit of Sir C.W. Domvile bt. for wilfully damaging and carrying away the thatch and timber of a cabin in which, subsequent to his being dispossessed as a tenant, he had been employed as a caretaker at 6d. per week ... The defendant pleaded, that as a number of other tenants on the estate, who had been similarly dispossessed of their holdings, had been allowed to pull down their dwellings, and carry portions of them away, and had also received money for giving up possession, he thought that he had been entitled to the same indulgence. He claimed 14s. as the wages for his services as caretaker ... The bench convicted the prisoner, and ordered the payment of 10s. fine, and 10s. costs, or imprisonment for one month.[31]

Another Shankill tenant evicted at this time was John McAneny, mentioned above, who lived at the bottom of Quarry Road and was evicted for quarrying stone on his land for road construction.[32] He, too, took on land at Tillystown. Others who moved to Tillystown were William Geelin, Edward Thomas, John Tierney and Peter Kearney, all from the Quarry Road area, John Butler from the western side of the mountain and Peter Toole, who had been evicted from the forge at Mullinastill on Tilly's land. Some time later Joseph Mills himself moved to live in Tillystown.[33] It is notable that no tenants from Rathmichael seem to have moved to Tillystown.

Those Shankill tenants who took land at Tillystown do not fit the stereotype of the evicted family. The houses built in Tillystown were more substantial than those the tenants had occupied at Shankill and a significant number of them built more than one house. Of 17 holders of property at Tillystown who are identifiable as having come from the Shankill estate, only 11 actually lived in the new village. The others held land, usually with at least one house let to tenants. John Butler came from a house in Shankill with a poor law valuation of 10s., and built six houses valued at £2 each, which he let to tenants. John McAneny's house at Shankill had had a valuation of 15s., and he built one at Tillystown valued at £7 and two others for renting. Edward Thomas built two houses for tenants and Charles Kearney moved from a house in Shankill with a valuation of £1 to one he built in Tillystown valued at £4, with a second one valued at £2 10s. let to a tenant. Every one of them occupied a house worth more than the old one in Shankill, generally worth twice the amount, sometimes more. Against this, the amount of land with each house was less, usually a quarter acre per house, whereas most of them had held small farms in Shankill.[34]

It is very puzzling how these evicted tenants could afford to provide themselves with better accommodation than they had prior to eviction. There are two possibilities – compensation and loans. W.E. Vaughan makes a convincing case for the existence of tenant right in certain instances in many parts of the country.³⁵ This would have given the tenant a degree of security of tenure and permitted the buying and selling of the tenancy and could attract payment of compensation if this right was infringed through eviction. There is no mention in the Domvile papers of any payments to tenants or any question of the existence of rights that may have required compensation, though the report of William Everard's eviction quoted above mentions that tenants had 'received money for giving up possession'. There is a possibility that loans could have been available from building societies; one had opened at Kingstown (Dun Laoghaire) at the beginning of 1862.³⁶ If this was the means of financing the new houses, it could have encouraged the construction of houses for tenants to provide a rental income to repay the loan. Whatever way the evicted tenants financed the construction of their houses, they, and the other new inhabitants, managed to build them in significant numbers. By 1871, there were 62 occupied houses in Tillystown and the population of the new village was well over 300.³⁷ By contrast, Shankill and Rathmichael townlands had a combined population of 241, with just 43 houses. By the end of the century Tillystown had nearly a 100 houses and had begun to form the nucleus for a larger village. As the village grew in the twentieth century the name Tillystown came to refer to just the part laid out by Benjamin Tilly, while the village as a whole took on the name of its railway station – Shankill – despite standing more in Shanganagh than Shankill townland.

In his attempted development of his Shankill estate, Sir Charles failed to attract new building, while he cleared out the old tenants, particularly those who were labourers or small farmers. It is a great irony that the most lasting effect of his work was that Shankill village moved off his land and that the resulting 70 houses or so that were built were for his lesser tenants and not the gentry. When the Rathdown labourers' cottages were built on the Shankill estate at New Vale, next to Tillystown, in 1911, many of the surnames were those of the evictees, such as Whelan, Doyle, Butler, Kavanagh, Geelon and Mason.³⁸ As Tillystown grew, Domvile's fortunes waned, and perhaps an indicator of this can be seen in the listings in *Thom's Directory*. Domvile was not listed in the earlier 1850s as he was resident in England. He appeared in the mid-1850s listed at 39 Gardiner Street Lower, Dublin and following his father's death his address became Santry House. By 1861, his addresses were Santry House, Hermitage in Howth, Boveridge Park in Dorset and Brook's club. In the following year Shankill was added to the list, while Hermitage changed to Evora, Howth, and this group of addresses remained in the listings until 1865. In 1866, he let Evora to a tenant and it no longer appeared in the directory. From 1867, Boveridge Park disappeared from the listing, followed by Shankill from 1870. From that date until 1875 Sir Charles was listed at Santry House and Brook's, following which he no longer appeared in *Thom's*

Directory.[39] His disappearance from the family home followed opinions sought as to the legality of letting the house to a tenant and subsequently selling it.[40] He then conveyed the mansion to his old friend and adversary Captain W.C. Caldwell.[41] Domvile was declared bankrupt in 1876.[42] According to Joseph Mills:

> Sir Charles died in France a bankrupt, it is believed he was out of his mind; his successor, Mr William Domvile, only lived three weeks; and his son, who inherited after him again, was an idiot.[43]

Again, Mills is not correct in every detail. Sir Charles died in 1884, at the age of 61 and was succeeded by his brother William, who died 11 weeks later, at the age of 59.[44] Sir William Domvile had one son, Sir Compton Meade Domvile, who was of unsound mind, and was a ward of court for the full 50 years that he held the title.[45] As had happened previously, the Domviles died out in the male line with the death of Sir Compton Meade Domvile in 1935. Next in line was a son of one of Sir William's daughters, Sir Hugo Compton Domvile Poë. This heir apparent could inherit only if he changed his surname to Domvile and therein lay a problem. Like his uncle before him, he was of unsound mind, and the lawyers said that he could not inherit the estate as his name could not be changed for him and he was not capable of doing so himself. The only solution was an act of parliament or, as the estates were in Ireland, an act of the Oireachtas. With yet another irony, the nascent Irish Free State legislature passed the Poë Name and Arms (Compton Domvile Estates) Act, 1936 to enable the estate, once again, to be presided over by a baronet who was incapable of understanding his wealth and position.[46] In the closing sentence to his introduction, having related the fate of Sir Charles Domvile and his brother William, Joseph Mills simply wrote:

> The mills of God grind slowly, but they grind exceedingly small.[47]

Conclusion

Although direct evidence as to Sir Charles Domvile's character is not available, there is a significant amount of material which suggests that he could be unpleasant, impetuous, self-centred and uncaring. He also seems to have been incapable of understanding what was reasonable, and the instances with William Caldwell and with the Dublin County militia illustrate this point. Sir Charles' inability to grasp the implications of his actions may have been a factor in his financial dealings and his apparent enlarged sense of his own importance may have made it difficult for him to understand that anyone would dare to call in the debts and ruin him financially. In effect, his financial problems reflected two aspects of the same problem, both of which were linked to his character traits. Firstly, he mismanaged his borrowings, allowing them to grow until they bankrupted him. Secondly, he mismanaged his income. He was borrowing on the strength of future increased rents, but he lacked the ability to ensure that these increases came into effect. At Shankill, this was largely due to his inability to understand that in order to entice investors to acquire leases he would have to make his property more attractive than alternative properties such as at Bray, Foxrock or Killiney. He did not seem to be aware of free market conditions, and hence he discouraged potential lessees through onerous conditions on leases.

To be fair, the failure to attract builders of villas and terraces for the gentry was not entirely Sir Charles' fault. The opening of the Harcourt Street railway line made the land along its route more accessible to the city and should have resulted in development along its line. However, the demand did not materialize in the way that landowners had hoped. The best-known development along this line at the time was Foxrock which began in 1859 and within a few years had a hotel, a mart and a Church of Ireland church, as well as 30 villas.[1] However, this was well below the intended scale of the development, the enterprise failed and hence most of the houses in Foxrock today date from a generation later. On the lands of Shanganagh close to Shankill station, an adjoining landowner advertised sites for development in May 1863, but no sites were developed.[2] The difficulty of finding takers for his sites and the difficulties experienced by others should have made any business-minded proprietor aware of the need to gain a competitive edge. Sir Charles did not rise to this, however, and as has been seen in the case of the substantial house at Ballybride, he was unable to moderate his demands even in the face of losing two potential purchasers. The eviction of tenants or forcing them out through onerous clauses in leases or large rises in rents also show his failure to understand the effects of his actions on others. Eviction was, and remains, an essential tool in the management of property, but its use needs to be moderated to ensure that it is fair and is not employed unnecessarily. The gains which Domvile made at Shankill and Rathmichael were small in comparison with the effects his actions had on his tenants.

The degree to which the events at Shankill were influenced by the state of the economy or political climate of the time is unclear. This period was an important one in landlord-tenant relations as it lay in the lull between the Famine and the Land War. One writer has stated that 'by 1860 the power of the Irish landlord was at the zenith. He was enabled by law to dispose of his property as he saw fit.'[3] This situation ensured that Sir Charles Domvile was able to carry out evictions on grounds that would not have been sufficient a few years later as the later 19th century Land Acts came into play. On the other hand, it is possible that the agricultural depression of the early 1860s played a part in reducing the income of members of the gentry, or at least reducing the certainty of future income, thereby making the property market less attractive. Most people of wealth at the time held a great deal of their capital in land, even members of the professional classes, as they acquired investment property to provide the equivalent of pension income. While factors such as the legal and economic climate may have had some influence over the outcome of the events at Shankill in the late 1850s and into the 1860s, there is no doubt that the personality of Sir Charles Domvile also played a hugely significant role.

Notes

ABBREVIATIONS

Burke   Sir Bernard Burke, *Peerage and Baronetage* (London, 1890)
Cooper   Account book of W.J. Cooper
NLI, Domvile Domvile papers in the National Library of Ireland.
GO   Genealogical Office, Dublin
Mills   Joseph Mills, *Recollections of Shankill during the 'reign' of the exterminator, Sir Charles Domvile* (Shankill, Co. Dublin, 1906).
NA   National Archives of Ireland
NLI   National Library of Ireland
Peyton   Day book of Randle Peyton, solicitor
Rathdown indoor   Indoor relief books of the Board of Guardians of the Rathdown Union
Rathdown outdoor   Outdoor relief books of the Board of Guardians of the Rathdown Union
RD   Registry of Deeds, Henrietta Street, Dublin 1
Riall   Diary of Phineas Riall, in private possession
VOR   Valuation Office cancelled books for DED Rathmichael, Co. Dublin

INTRODUCTION

1 Peyton, 1857 (NLI, Domvile, MS 11868); Peyton, 1861–62 (NLI, Domvile, MS 11826); Cooper 1864–9 (NLI, Domvile, MS 11825).
2 For listings of maps see R.J. Hayes, (ed.) *Manuscript sources for the history of Irish civilisation* (11 vols, Boston, 1965) vii, p. 500.
3 Mills.
4 In the census returns for 1901 and 1911 Mills' education is recorded as 'Read only' (NA, census 1901, D.E.D. 89/16c, form A; census 1911, D.E.D. 87/16, form A).
5 NA microfiche reference 6 E 13.
6 VOR, townlands of Shankill and Rathmichael.
7 The *Bray Gazette* is available on microfilm in the National Library of Ireland for the years 1861–9.
8 Census 1901 (NA, D.E.D. 89/13, 15 and 16c, microfilm); Census 1911, (NA, D.E.D. 87/13, 15 and 16, microfilm).
9 Rathdown indoor (NA, BG137 G1 to G45); Rathdown outdoor (NA, BG 137 EA1).

1. BACKGROUND: THE DOMVILES AND SHANKILL

1 Pedigree of Domvile and Compton Domvile, barts. and Pocklington (later Domvile) of city of Dublin and Leighlinstown and of Lyme, Cheshire and St Albans, Hertfordshire, 1066–1814 (NLI, GO, MS 170, pp 247–253).
2 Burke, pp 423–4.
3 R.C. Simington, *The civil survey AD 1654–1656: vii. county of Dublin* (Dublin 1945), p. 269; F.E. Ball, *A history of the Co. Dublin, part first* (Dublin, 1902, facsimile edition 1979) pp 89, 90–91.
4 E.M. Johnston-Liik, *History of the Irish parliament 1692–1800* (6 vols, Belfast, 2002), vi, p. 72.
5 Burke pp 378–9.
6 Pedigree of Domvile.
7 Pedigree of Domvile; Johnston-Liik, *History of the Irish parliament*, iv, p. 70; Ball, *Co. Dublin, part first* p. 93.
8 Burke, pp 423–4.
9 Pedigree of Domvile, Burke, pp 423–4.

10 Pedigree of Domvile.
11 Compton C. Domvile to Charles C.W. Domvile, 26 Nov. [?year] (NLI, Domvile, MS 11854) Many of the letters do not include the year in the date, and as they are not filed in any logical sequence there is no way of knowing the year in the absence of internal evidence.
12 Compton C. Domvile to Charles C.W. Domvile, 22 Sept. [?year, c.1849] (NLI, Domvile, MS 11854).
13 Helena Domvile to Charles C.W. Domvile, 9 July [?year, c.1849] (NLI, Domvile, MS 11854).
14 Capt. W. Caldwell to Charles C.W. Domvile, 24 Nov. [1849], 19 Apr. 1850, 5 July 1850, 15 July 1850 and 25 July 1850 (NLI, Domvile, MS 11854).
15 *Thom's Directory*, 1856, p. 411.
16 Lord Meath to Major C.C.W. Domvile (NLI, Domvile, MS 11857).
17 Major C.C.W. Domvile to Lord Meath, n.d. [1856]; Major C.C.W. Domvile to Major General Eden, 5 Feb. 1856 (NLI, Domvile, MS 11857).
18 Newspaper cutting reporting meeting of board of guardians of North Dublin union, 31 Jan. 1857, source of cutting not recorded (NLI, Domvile, MS 9395).
19 Burke, pp 423–4.
20 RD, 1842/3/210; 1842/14/250.
21 RD, 1842/20/62.
22 Opinion of Mr Loftus Wigram, 27 July 1852 (NLI, Domvile, MS 11811).
23 Law costs, 19 July 1852 (NLI, Domvile, MS 11811).
24 RD, 1854/26/169.
25 John Buller, 'Counsel's opinion on second Domvile Estate Act' 21 Jan. 1862 (NLI, Domvile, MS 11769); 67 architectural drawings, mainly for Santry (NLI, Architectural drawings, AD2385–2425, AD2427–2461 and AD3427; AD1574–1586; AD3310, AD3426).
26 Rentals of the Domvile estate, 1857–1871 (NLI, Domvile, MS 11819).
27 Figures compiled from acreages given in the Valuation Office cancelled books and rents given in estate rentals (NLI, Domvile, MS 11819) and Charles Toole's list of tenants (NLI, Domvile, MS 11799).
28 Extracts from applications for presentment for the building and repair of public roads at Rathmichael and Shankill 9 April 1860 (NLI, Domvile, MS 11776); agreement between Sir C.C.W. Domvile and Edward Hanven of Shankill, 13 September 1858 (NLI, Domvile, MS 11777). This refers to property alongside 'the new road at Shankill lately made by or at the expense of Sir Compton Domvile leading from Rathmichael to Frompstown'.
29 James Fraser, *Report on Shankill, the estate of Sir C.C.W. Domvile Baronet as adapted to demesne and villa allotments planting and other improvements* (NLI, Domvile, MS 11803 (8)).
30 Fraser, *Report on Shankill*.
31 James Fraser, *Map of part of Shankill, Co. Dublin, the property of Sir C.C.W. Domvile, showing proposed deposition of ground for terrace and villa lots* n.d. (NLI, Domvile, 16 G 42 (21)).
32 VOR, Shankill townland, volume 1, book 3.
33 Ibid.
34 Ordnance Survey 1:2500 Dublin sheet 26–10 (n.d.).
35 VOR, Rathmichael townland, volume 1, book 3, plots 15, 16, 17 and 18.
36 Ibid., book 4, plot 14.
37 Ibid., book 3, plot 15.
38 VOR, Shankill townland, volume 1, book 3, plots 72, 73, 74 and 75.
39 Rentals of Dublin estates (NLI, Domvile, MS 11819).
40 Evidence of Joseph Kincaid to the judges appointed to hear the petition in favour of the Domvile Estate Bill 1860. (NLI, Domvile, MS 11797).
41 Settled Estates Act, 1857, 19 & 20 Vic. c.120.
42 Thomas de Moleyns, *The landed property improvement and landlord and tenant consolidation acts* (Dublin, 1860), p. 13.
43 Opinion of Francis F.L. Dames, 29 May 1860 (NLI, Domvile, MS 11798(5)).
44 R Peyton to F.F.L. Dames, n.d. (NLI, Domvile, MS 11798(6)).
45 Opinion of F.F.L. Dames, 2 Jan. 1860 (NLI, Domvile, MS 11798(11)).
46 Invitation to attend hearing (NLI, Domvile, MS 11798(4)).
47 Transcript of hearing of 5 July 1860 (NLI, Domvile, MS 11798(7)).
48 Edward C. Carleton to Brassington and Gale, 14 Apr. 1860 (NLI, Domvile, MS 11798 (10)).
49 Copy of opinion of Messrs Brassington and Geale (*sic*), 12 April 1860 (NLI, Domvile, MS 11798(3)).
50 Professional title as listed in *Thom's Directory* for 1861.
51 Opinion of Joseph Jas. Byrne, 30 April 1860 (NLI, Domvile, MS 11798(2)).

52 Evidence taken before the judges relating to Domvile Estate Act, 1860, 8 June 1860 (NLI, Domvile, MS 11797).
53 Ibid.
54 Domvile Estate Act, 1860, 33 & 34 Vic. Ch. 6.
55 Ibid., clause I, pp 199–201.
56 Ibid., clause II, p. 201.
57 Ibid., clauses XIV and XV, page 205.

2. IMPLEMENTATION

1 *London Morning Chronicle*, 10 Apr. 1860.
2 *Freeman's Journal*, 17 Apr. 1860.
3 *London Morning Chronicle*, 10 Apr. 1860; *Freeman's Journal*, 17 Apr. 1860; General account book 1861–69, 15 Mar. 1860 (NLI, Domvile, MS 11839).
4 *London Morning Chronicle*, 10 Apr. 1860.
5 Riall, 16 Apr 1860.
6 Peyton, 14 Jan. 1861 (NLI, Domvile, MS 11826).
7 VOR, townland of Shanganagh and Shankill.
8 VOR, townlands of Rathmichael and Ballycorus.
9 Peyton, 24 Jan., 21 and 25 Mar., 2 Sept, 7 and 30 Oct. and 11 Nov. 1861 (NLI, Domvile, MS 11826).
10 Peyton, 13 and 22 Jan. and 15 Feb. 1858 (NLI, Domvile, MS 11868).
11 Legal opinion re Mining Company of Ireland, n.d. (NLI, Domvile, MS 11807); Peyton, 11 Feb and 8 Mar. 1858 (NLI, Domvile, MS 11868).
12 Peyton, 16 Mar. 1858 (NLI, Domvile, MS 11868); VOR, townland of Rathmichael; Legal opinion re Mining Company of Ireland, n.d. (NLI, Domvile, MS 11807).
13 *Bray Gazette*, 4 Jan. 1862.
14 'An illiberal act toward a liberal voter' n.d. (NLI, Domvile, MS 9395).
15 *Bray Gazette*, 25 October 1862.
16 K. Turner, *If you seek monuments* (Dublin, 1983), pp 55–9; K. Turner, *Rathmichael: A parish history* (Dublin, 1988), pp 29–30.
17 Peyton, 5 Apr. 1858 (NLI, Domvile, MS 11868).
18 Deeds, 1860/3/295.
19 F. O'Dwyer, *The architecture of Deane and Woodward* (Cork, 1997), pp 502–7.
20 Peyton, 4 Mar. 1861 (NLI, Domvile, MS 11826).
21 Peyton, 5 Mar. 1861 (ibid.).
22 O'Dwyer, *The architecture of Deane and Woodward*, p. 506.
23 Peyton, 8 and 14 Aug. 1861 (NLI, Domvile, MS 11826).
24 Peyton, 27 Aug. 1861 (NLI, Domvile, MS 11826); C.H. Holland (ed.), *Trinity College Dublin & the idea of a university* (Dublin 1991), p. 300.
25 Peyton, 11 Oct. 1861 (NLI, Domvile, MS 11826).
26 O'Dwyer, *Architecture of Deane and Woodward*, p. 506.
27 Riall, 16 Mar. 1862.
28 O'Dwyer, *Architecture of Deane and Woodward*, p. 507.
29 Riall, 26 Aug. 1866.
30 Turner, *Rathmichael*, p. 31.
31 Fraser, *Report on Shankill*.
32 VOR, townland of Shankill.
33 Ibid.
34 Ibid.
35 Riall, 8 and 28 Oct. and 16 Nov. 1860.
36 Accounts of Benjamin T. Patterson ICE Surveyor (Irish Architectural Archive, PKS 77/1/A3, ledger no. 1, cash book).
37 http://www2.cr.nps.gov/tps/roofingexhibit/metals.htm, viewed on 16 June 2002.
38 'Iron buildings', *Dublin Builder*, ii, 1 June 1860, p. 270; 'Corrugated iron buildings', *Manufacturer and Builder*, i (Dec. 1869).
39 Unlabelled drawing (NLI, architectural drawings, AD 2440).
40 Stable yard (NLI, architectural drawings, AD 2448).
41 Tenancy of iron cottage at entrance to Racefields, 1869 (NLI, Domvile, MS 11322).
42 Galvanised corrugated iron cottage (NLI, architectural drawings, AD 2453).
43 Ibid.; this drawing is labelled with Morton's name and address; Domvile Estate Act, 1868, schedule (C).
44 *Bray Gazette*, 30 Aug. 1862.
45 Niven's report is headed 'Statement to Sir Charles W Domvile Bart. in reply to letters of dates 30 Aug., 4 and 11 Sept. 1862' (NLI, Domvile, MS 11803).
46 K. Lamb and P. Bowe, *A history of gardening in Ireland* (Dublin, 1995), pp 110–17.
47 Niven, 'Statement'.
48 James Douglass vs. Sir C.C.W. Domvile (NLI, Domvile, MS 11787).
49 RD, 610/196/419754.
50 RD, 676/107/465804.
51 RD, 619/475/425061.
52 None of these houses appears on Duncan's map of Co. Dublin of 1821, while all appear in S. Lewis' *Topographical dictionary of Ireland* (3 vols, London, 1837) under 'Rathmichael'.
53 Peyton, 30 Mar. 1858 (NLI, Domvile, MS 11868).
54 Peyton, 14 Mar. 1861 (NLI, Domvile, MS 11826).
55 Peyton, 21 Mar. to 10 Apr. 1861 (NLI, Domvile, MS 11826).

56 List of tenancies returned by Mr Toole on 10 May 1861 (NLI, Domvile, MS 11799).
57 Ibid.
58 RD, 1861/28/177.
59 Lists of occupiers on Toole's land, 10 May 1861 (NLI, Domvile, MS 11799); VOR, townland of Shankill.
60 VOR, townland of Shankill.
61 Mills, pp 11–13.
62 List of tenancies, 10 May 1861 (NLI, Domvile, MS 11799).
63 VOR, townlands of Shanganagh and Shankill.
64 Peyton, 14 and 24 Jan., 11 Feb., 1 Mar. 1861 (NLI, Domvile, MS 11826).
65 Peyton, 27 Aug. 1861 (NLI, Domvile, MS 11826); List of tenants of Charles Toole 10 May 1861 (NLI, Domvile, MS 11799).
66 Peyton, 30 Aug., 2 and 17 Sept., 30 Oct., 9, 11, 15, 18, 25 Nov. 1861, 9 and 16 Jan. 1862 (NLI, Domvile, MS 11826).
67 Peyton, 4 Apr. 1862 (NLI, Domvile, MS 11826).
68 Peyton, 5 Apr. 1862 (NLI, Domvile, MS 11868).
69 VOR, townland of Shankill.
70 Peyton, 20 Mar. 1862 (NLI, Domvile, MS 11826).
71 VOR, townland of Shankill. This assessment excludes the six gatelodges on Toole's land which cannot be examined in the same way as the valuation records do not tend to note the names of their occupiers.
72 Peyton, 11 Nov. 1861 (NLI, Domvile, MS 11826).
73 Peyton, 18 Dec. 1861 (ibid.).
74 Rentals of the city and county of Dublin, Sept. 1864 (NLI, Domvile, MS 11819).
75 Fraser, *Report on Shankill*.
76 Based on the houses named on the first edition Ordnance Survey six-inch sheet Dublin 26, 1843.
77 VOR, townlands of Rathmichael and Shankill.
78 VOR, townland of Rathmichael; Mills, p. 7.
79 Mills, pp 11, 4.
80 VOR, townland of Shankill.
81 VOR, townland of Rathmichael.
82 Peyton, 19 Jan. 1858 (NLI, Domvile, MS 11868).
83 Peyton, 19, 22 Jan., 15 Feb., 2, 8, 16, 26 Mar., 1, 18, 25 May 1858 (NLI, Domvile, MS 11868); Peyton, 23, 27 July, 2, 15 Aug. 1861, 8 Jan. 1862 (NLI, Domvile, MS 11826).
84 VOR, townlands of Rathmichael and Shankill.
85 Edward Jones' case in *Fowler v. Domvile* (NLI, Domvile, MS 11807); Mills, p. 11; VOR, townland of Shankill.
86 VOR, townland of Shankill.
87 Peyton, 30 Dec. 1857 (NLI, Domvile, MS 11868).
88 Costs of case defending ejectment in *Sir C.C.W. Domvile v. Anne Isabella Fowler and others*, Mar. 1858 and affidavit of Mary Byrne in *Sir C.C.W. Domvile v. Anne Isabella Fowler and others*, 19 Mar. 1858 (NLI, Domvile, MS 11787); VOR, townland of Shankill.
89 VOR, townland of Shankill; Mills, p. 11.
90 Peyton, 13 Sept. 1862 (ibid., MS 11826).
91 Peyton, 31 Dec. 1861 (ibid.).
92 Peyton, 17 Sept. 1862 (ibid.).
93 Peyton, 4 and 13 Dec. 1862 (ibid.).
94 VOR, townland of Rathmichael.
95 Newspaper cutting, source and date not recorded (NLI, Domvile, MS 9395).
96 Thomas de Moleyns, *The landowner's and agent's practical guide* (Dublin, 1860), p. 22.
97 Ibid., p. 24.
98 Ibid., pp 22–3.
99 Mills, p. 9.
100 *Bray Gazette*, 27 Sept. 1862; rentals of the city and county of Dublin, Sept. 1861 to Sept. 1862 (NLI, Domvile, MS 11819).
101 Case of Sir C.C.W. Domvile re the lands of Kilternan (sic), (NLI, Domvile, MS 11769).
102 RD, 1858/22/272.
103 Case of Sir C.C.W. Domvile re lands at Kilternan (sic) (NLI, Domvile, MS 11769).
104 Peyton, 4 Aug. 1862 (NLI, Domvile, MS 11826).
105 Ibid.
106 W. E. Vaughan, *Landlords and tenants in mid-Victorian Ireland* (Oxford 1994), pp 142, 150–6.
107 Peyton, 23 Aug. 1862 (NLI, Domvile, MS 11826).
108 Peyton, 26 Aug. 1862 (NLI, Domvile, MS 11826).
109 Peyton, 27 Aug. 1862 (ibid.).
110 Ibid.
111 Peyton, 28 Aug. 1862 (ibid.).
112 Peyton, 15 and 29 Sept. 1862 (ibid.).
113 Peyton, 13 and 29 Nov. 1862 (ibid.).
114 Chief Secretary's Office register, 29 Oct. 1862 (NA).
115 Peyton, 5 Nov. 1862 (NLI, Domvile, MS 11826); Chief Secretary's Office Registered Papers, 29 Oct. 1862 (NA, CSORP 19259). This item is missing from the collection of the NA.
116 'Arrest of the supposed writer of the threatening letter to Mr Garnett', newspaper cutting, no source, story dated 'Roscommon Sept. 6th 1862' (NLI, Domvile, MS 9395).

117 Peyton, 12, 13 and 16 Sept. 1862 (NLI, Domvile, MS 11826).
118 Report dated 18 Sept. 1862, (NLI, Domvile, MS 11788).
119 Peyton, 30 Aug. 1862 (NLI, Domvile, MS 11826)
120 Peyton, 2 Sept. 1862 (ibid.).
121 Peyton, 26 and 27 Sept. 1862 (ibid.).
122 Peyton, 1 and 2 Oct. 1862 (ibid.).
123 Peyton, 2 and 3 Oct. 1862 (ibid.).
124 Peyton, 20 and 18 Oct. 1862 (ibid.).
125 *Sir Charles Domvile and others v. John Brack and others*, nisi prius court, 9 Jan. 1863 (NLI, Domvile, MS 11776).
126 Riall, 20 Dec. 1862.
127 Sir Charles Domvile and others v. Thomas Doyle and others, nisi prius court, 9 Jan. 1863 (ibid.).
128 Ibid.
129 VOR, townland of Rathmichael.
130 Rentals of the city and county of Dublin, Sept. 1866 (NLI, Domvile, MS 11819).
131 Notice of trial, Sir Charles C.W. Domvile Bt., plaintiff and John Brack defendant (NLI, Domvile, MS 11319 (2)); Landlord and Tenant Act (Ireland), 1860.
132 *Freeman's Journal*, 20 Jan. 1864.
133 *Irishman*, 23 Jan. 1864, p. 473.
134 Rentals of the city and county of Dublin, Sept. 1866 and Mar. 1871 (NLI, Domvile, MS 11819).
135 Mills, p. 8.
136 Ordnance Survey six-inch Dublin sheet 26, 1843 and manuscript valuation maps in the Valuation Office.

3. SUCCESS OR FAILURE?

1 *Bray Gazette*, 15 June 1861.
2 RD, 1862/21/105; legal opinion re compensation claim of Sarah Doyle (NLI, Domvile, MS 11807).
3 VOR, townland of Shankill.
4 Peyton, 9 July and 30 Aug. 1861, 5 Feb. 1862 (NLI, Domvile, MS 11826).
5 RD, 1865/28/215. This is a deed of mortgage which recites the earlier deed of 21 Dec. 1863.
6 Rentals of the city and county of Dublin, Mar. 1864 (NLI, Domvile, MS 11819).
7 VOR, townland of Shankill.
8 Cooper, 15 Aug. 1864 (NLI, Domvile, MS 11825).
9 Ibid., 22 Dec. 1864.
10 Cooper, 31 Jan. 1865 (ibid.).
11 Cooper, 5 and 9 Jan. and 10 Mar. 1866 (ibid.).
12 Cooper, 12 Mar. 1866 (ibid.).
13 Cooper, 22 Mar. 1866 (ibid.).
14 Cooper, 4 Apr. 1866 (ibid.).
15 Cooper, 25 May 1866 (ibid.).
16 Cooper, 5 Apr. 1866 (ibid.).
17 Cooper, 7 June 1866 (ibid.).
18 Cooper, 31 Jan and 28 Feb. 1867 (ibid.).
19 Cooper, 23 Mar. 1866 (ibid.).
20 VOR, townland of Shankill.
21 Ibid.
22 Ibid.
23 Ibid.
24 Ibid. shows changes to valuation of buildings denoting where new buildings were erected or existing ones enlarged.
25 Ibid.
26 Peyton, 26 Nov. 1857 (NLI, Domvile, MS 11868).
27 Peyton, 4 Mar. 1861 (ibid.).
28 Peyton, 18 Mar. 1861 (ibid.).
29 Peyton, 22 Mar. 1861 (ibid.).
30 Peyton, 6 July 1861 (ibid.).
31 Peyton, 23 Dec. 1861 (ibid.).
32 Peyton, 26 Dec. 1861 (ibid.).
33 Peyton, 8 July 1862 (ibid.).
34 Peyton, 9 Aug. 1862 (ibid.).
35 RD, 1852/17/11.
36 Peyton, 30 Dec. 1861 (NLI, Domvile, MS 11826).
37 Peyton, 11 Jan. 1862 (ibid.).
38 Peyton, 17, 18 and 20 Jan. 1862 (ibid.).
39 Peyton, 15 Jan. 1861 (ibid.).
40 James Mackey later served two terms as lord mayor of Dublin in 1866–7 and 1872–3 and was knighted in 1874 (Dod's *Peerage, baronetage and knightage of Great Britain and Ireland*, London, 1883).
41 Peyton, 19 Dec. 1861; 3 Jan., 1 and 3 July 1862 (NLI, Domvile, MS 11826).
42 Peyton, 8 and 20 Aug. 1862 (ibid.).
43 Cooper, 18 Jan. 1865 (NLI, Domvile, MS 11825).
44 RD, 1865/34/200; VOR, townland of Shankill.
45 VOR, townland of Shankill.
46 RD, 1869/18/101.
47 *Sir C.C.W. Domvile vs. William C. Domvile* (NLI, Domvile, MS 11769).
48 Letter to Mr Spencer enclosing notice to quit for Mr Wm. Domvile (NLI, Domvile, MS 11826).
49 Peyton, 15 Oct. 1862 (ibid.).
50 Cooper, 6 Sept. 1864, 8 Dec. 1864 and 11 Apr. 1865 (NLI, Domvile, MS 11825).
51 Rentals of the city and county of Dublin, Sept. 1863 (NLI, Domvile, MS 11819).
52 Report dated 18 Sept. 1862, (NLI, Domvile, MS 11788).
53 Brassington and Gale, *Map of part of the estate of Sir Compton Domvile bt. in the county of Dublin*, 1854 (NLI, 21 F 102).

54 Ordnance Survey, six-inch Dublin sheet 26, 1871.
55 The calculation of the length of fences excludes the townland boundary and includes roads and lanes, counting these as a single length of fence without taking each side as a separate fence.
56 Rentals of the city and county of Dublin, Sept. 1862 (NLI, Domvile, MS 11819).
57 Richard A. Gray, *Specification for the erection of farm dwelling and offices at Shankill, Co. Dublin, part of the estate of Sir Charles C.W. Domvile, Bart.* (NLI, Domvile, MS 11803).
58 Sandham Symes, architect, *Design for farm offices to be built at Shankill on the estate of Sir Charles C.W. Domvile, Bart.* (NLI, AD 2455).
59 *James Douglass v Sir C.C.W. Domvile*, (NLI, Domvile, MS 11787).
60 VOR, townland of Shankill.
61 Ordnance Survey six-inch Dublin sheet 26, 1871.
62 *Dublin Builder*, vii, (15 Feb. 1865), p. 51.
63 Mills p. 10.
64 Peyton, 9 Apr. 1861(NLI, Domvile, MS 11826).
65 *Bray Gazette*, 27 July 1861.
66 As per n.53 (NLI, 21 F 102).
67 Annual Reports of the Mining Company of Ireland (NLI Ir622 m3).
68 'Application … for the making of a new road twenty-five feet in the clear … two hundred and twenty-seven perches long …' (NLI, Domvile, MS 11776).
69 Articles of agreement, Sept. 1860 (NLI, Domvile, MS 11789).
70 R. Peyton account with Sir C.C. Domvile, 1 May to 31 Oct. 1860 (NLI, Domvile, MS 11787).
71 Virginia Crossman, *Local government in nineteenth-century Ireland* (Belfast, 1994), p. 27.
72 *Freeman's Journal*, 17 Apr. 1860.
73 Domvile Estate Act, 1868, 31 & 32 Vict., schedule (C). This contains a list of expenditure, including the purpose and to whom it was paid. Whether this was expended at Santry or at Shankill is normally specified, but where it is not the context suggests that it was at Santry.
74 John Buller, counsel's opinion on second Domvile Estate Act, 21 Jan. 1862 (NLI, Domvile, MS 11769).
75 Domvile Estate Act, 1868, 31 & 32 Vict., schedule (C).
76 Rentals of the city and county of Dublin, Sept. 1857 (NLI, Domvile, MS 11819).
77 Rentals of the city and county of Dublin, Mar. 1871 (ibid.).
78 Toole's tenants, 10 May 1861 (NLI, Domvile, MS 11799).
79 Rentals of the city and county of Dublin, Mar. 1871 (NLI, Domvile, MS 11819).
80 Vaughan, *Landlords and tenants in mid-Victorian Ireland*, p. 239.
81 John Buller, counsel's opinion on second Domvile Estate Act, 21 Jan. 1862 (NLI, Domvile, MS 11769)
82 William Domvile to Charles Domvile, May 1849 and William Caldwell to Charles Domvile, 24 Nov. [1849] (NLI, Domvile, MS 11854).
83 RD, 1858/1/99.
84 RD, 1858/2/242, 1859/3/134, 1859/10/250 and 1859/9/164.
85 RD, 1862/1/197, 1862/23/144, 1862/36/168, 1862/27/209, 1863/3/283, 1862/27/209, 1863/3/283 and 1863/10/147.
86 RD, 1863/3/283 cites various insurance. There are frequent mentions in W.J. Cooper's accounts of insurance policies being offered to lenders or creditors, see NLI, MS 11825.
87 RD, 1863/15/85, 1863/34/122, 1864/9/157 and 1863/37/159.
88 RD, 1864/26/135 and 1864/26/136.
89 Peyton (NLI, Domvile, MS 11868 and MS 11826); Cooper (NLI, Domvile, MS 11825).
90 Cooper (NLI, Domvile, MS 11825); occupations from H. Shaw, *The Dublin pictorial guide and directory of 1850* (Dublin 1850, reprinted Belfast, 1988).
91 Cooper, 26 July 1865, 13 Jan 1866 and 16 Nov 1864 (NLI, Domvile, MS 11825).
92 Cooper, 30 Jan. 1866 (ibid.).
93 Cooper, 7 Sept. 1864 and 20 Jan. 1866 (NLI, Domvile, MS 11825).
94 Cooper, 25 Jan. 1866 (ibid.).
95 Cooper, 3 Jan. 1866, 3 Feb. 1866 (ibid.).
96 Cooper, 5 Feb. 1866 (ibid.).
97 Cooper, 30 July 1866 (ibid.).
98 Cooper, 10 Apr. 1866 (ibid.).
99 Cooper, 16 Oct. and 5 Nov. 1866 (ibid.).
100 RD, 1866/32/233.
101 RD, 1866/33/106; 1866/33/203; 1866/34/3; 1866/33/275; 1866/33/276; 1866/34/109; 1866/34/110; 1866/34/111; 1866/34/263; 1866/35/184.
102 Cooper, 4 Dec. 1866 and 3 Jan. 1867 (NLI, Domvile, MS 11825).
103 John Buller, counsel's opinion on second Domvile Estate Act, 21 Jan. 1862 (NLI, Domvile, MS 11769).
104 Ibid.
105 Domvile Estate Act, 1868, 31 & 32 Vict. (the act bears no chapter number).

106 Ibid., section 1, Deeds, 1868/39/19.
107 RD, for example: 1867/3/245, 1867/6/267, 1867/8/37, 1868/38/19, 1869/7/86, 1872/25/26, 1873/15/161, 1874/5/112, 1874/21/55
108 RD, 1876/35/120.
109 Vaughan, Landlords and tenants, pp 130–7.
110 Encumbered Estates Act, 1849, 12 & 13 Vic. c. 77, section xxii.
111 Vaughan, Landlords and tenants, pp 131–3.

4. CONSEQUENCES

1 Census of Ireland, 1871, table VII, p. 77.
2 Opinion re Mining Company of Ireland (NLI, Domvile, MS 11807); VOR, townland of Rathmichael.
3 Census 1871, table VII, page 77.
4 VOR, townland of Rathmichael, for tenancies and areas.
5 VOR, townland of Rathmichael.
6 VOR, townlands of Rathmichael and Shankill.
7 Mills.
8 Vaughan, Landlords and tenants, p. 23.
9 Patrick Fallon, hon. secretary to the Dysart Relief Committee, in Roscommon Messenger undated cutting (NLI, Domvile, MS 9395).
10 Bray Gazette, 12 Apr. 1862.
11 Bray Gazette, 17 May 1862.
12 Bray Gazette, 31 Jan. 1863.
13 Bray Gazette, 15 Nov. 1862.
14 M. Timmons, 'The Vartry reservoir, Roundwood' in Blackrock Society Proceedings ii (1993–4), pp 48–55.
15 Bray Gazette, 31 Jan. 1863.
16 Bray Gazette, 7 Mar. 1863.
17 J. O'Connor, The workhouses of Ireland (Dublin, 1995), p. 179.
18 Peyton, 13 Nov. 1862 (NLI, Domvile, MS 11826); Rathdown indoor (NA, BG 137 G12).
19 Rathdown indoor (NA, BG 137 G12).
20 VOR, townland of Shankill.
21 Ibid.
22 Rathdown indoor (NA, BG 137 G13).
23 Ibid.
24 VOR, townland of Rathmichael; RBG indoor (NA, BG 137 G9).
25 Rathdown outdoor (NA, BG 137 EA1).
26 Mills, p. 16.
27 VOR, townland of Shanganagh.
28 RD, 1864/11/163; 1864/21/13; 1866/36/171; 1867/6/97.
29 Sir Charles Domvile and others vs. John Brack and others, nisi prius court, 9 Jan. 1863 ... (NLI, Domvile, MS 11776); Riall, 20 Dec. 1862.
30 VOR, townland of Shankill.
31 Bray Gazette, 9 May 1863.
32 VOR, townland of Shankill; Domvile vs. McAneny (NLI, Domvile, MS 11776).
33 VOR, townland of Shankill.
34 VOR, townlands of Shankill and Shanganagh.
35 Vaughan, Landlords and tenants in mid-Victorian Ireland (Oxford 1994), pp 67–102.
36 Dublin Builder iv, (1862), p. 33.
37 Census of population, 1871, Rathdown Barony, Rathmichael Parish, Tillytown.
38 VOR, townland of Shankill; Census of Population, 1901, Form A, Village of Tillystown, D.E.D. Rathmichael (NA).
39 Thom's Directory, 1850 to 1876.
40 Opinion as to whether land bill allows limited owner to let his mansion house on lease (NLI, Domvile, MS 11806).
41 Conveyance of land at Santry (NLI, Domvile, MS 11319 (2)).
42 RD, 1876/35/120.
43 Mills, p. 4.
44 Burke, pp 423–4.
45 See, for example, Deeds 1889/23/166; 1893/47/66; 1907/39/84.
46 Poë Name and Arms (Compton Domvile Estates) Act, 1936, No. 1 of 1936 (Private).
47 Mills, p. 4.

CONCLUSION

1 Douglas Bennett, Encyclopaedia of Dublin (Dublin, 1991), p. 80.
2 Bray Gazette, 23 May 1863; VOR, townland of Shanganagh.
3 John E. Pomfret, The struggle for land in Ireland, 1800–1923 (Princeton, 1930), quoted in W.E. Vaughan, Landlords and tenants in Ireland 1848–1904 (Dundalk, 1984), p. 13. Vaughan shows that Pomfret's conclusions were inaccurate in relation to rent levels and evictions. However, the statement quoted here is reasonable, the fault lying with drawing a conclusion
from it that landlords as a whole were unreasonable in the exercise of that power.